Praise for *Your Inner Knowing*

Neroli Makim brings to the world a masterpiece! This powerful book holds the wisdom to unleash your creative genius. Neroli's pictures speak to the soul, reminding you of your ability to be, do and have all that you want in life. Believing in your true potential is where it begins and this book supports your vision to create an amazing life."

—Starr Shephard
Internationally acclaimed motivational speaker and author

"This is a powerful book to help you discover and realise your personal creativity, that EVERYONE has inside of them. I truly believe Greatness is in all of us. Greatness is not this wonderful, illusive, God-like feature that only the special among us will ever taste. It's something that truly exists in all of us, and Neroli will show you how to discover yours in this wonderful book."

—Selina Scoble
Success coach and Olympian

"Neroli explains beautifully how to nurture, cultivate and grow an idea so that you may enjoy the success and fruition of your natural creativity. A sheer joy to read that will spark your inner wisdom and imagination that is so important in today's age of new opportunities for all humanity."

—Tracey Stranger
Speaker and author of *How to Overcome Stress Naturally*

"Neroli writes with the joy, enthusiasm and sensitivity of a child, whilst mingling this with her own extraordinary wisdom and that of some of the leading experts on creativity and self realisation on our planet today. She takes you through the most delightful and simple explanations and processes to uncover your unique form of creative expression. I can't wait to see more of her work!"

—Jo Woodham
Entrepreneur and holistic health consultant

Your Inner Knowing

Unlocking the Secrets

to Creative
Success

Disclaimer

The author is not rendering professional advice to the reader. The ideas, procedures and suggestions in this book are not intended as a substitute for consulting with a physician. All matters regarding health require medical supervision. The author shall not be liable or responsible for any loss or damage allegedly arising from and information or suggestions in this book. While the author has made every effort to provide accurate websites and Internet addresses at the time of publication, the author does not assume responsibility for errors or changes that occur after publication.

First published 2010
This edition published by LightGlobe Books 2011
www.YourCreativeSuccess.com

Copyright © 2010 Neroli Makim

National Library of Australia Cataloguing-in-Publication entry:
A catalogue record for this book is available from the National Library of Australia

Makim, Neroli
Your Inner Knowing
Unlocking the Secrets to Creative Success

1st ed.
ISBN: 978-0-9871405-0-0 (pbk)   Your Inner Knowing
1. Creative ability   2. Personality and creative ability   3. Self-actualisation (Psychology)

This book is dedicated to the creativity in every individual. You are gifted in a way that no one else on this planet is. The real secret is finding out how. The world needs your gifts; we're waiting for you to share them with us.

Neroli Makim

Special thanks

Dearest Mum, Dad and Haydn, thank you so much for loving and trusting in me enough to support me on this creative adventure even when it took a massive leap of faith. This book wouldn't be in print if it wasn't for you three.

Michael Leunig, thank you for the gentle insights and wise guidance in your artwork and the much needed inspiration and giggles that I get from your creative expression.

Anastasia, thank you for reminding me who I am and why I'm here, and thank you for finding the loophole ;)

Dr Stuart Brown, thank you for your dedication to your life's work that makes sense of my dedication to my life's play.

Dr John Demartini, thank you for being inspirational and for all the love and wisdom you share everyday.

Hugh MacLeod, thank you for telling it like it is, making me laugh and being a big inspiration for my creative expression.

 Ramy Youssef, thank you for being a gifted and intuitive photographer and artist to work with and for taking amazing pictures for my book and website.

Carla McKeever, thank you for being a gorgeous and talented makeup artist and helping me look fabulous in my photos.

Jacinta Makim, love you for being my wardrobe manager, style consultant, catering and location manager for my photo shoot, and for being my lovely sister.

Airdrie Makim, love you for being my marketing genius, press consultant and darling sister.

All other Makim siblings, Dom, Yooby, Ogga and Ijit (Dominic, Liam, Rod and Brigid) love you all lots, life is great when we're all together eating chocolate. Fran Kerr, big hug and thank you for all your kindness and generosity and for being a big catalyst in the creative direction of this book.

Yaro Starak, for the gift of directing me to Hugh MacLeod's work and for being a catalyst in the creative direction of this book, thank you.

Gideon Schalwick and Kerwin Rae, thank you so much for showing me by example that if you say you're going to do something, and then act on it, your dreams are within reach.

Thank you to the lovely children I've had the privilege and pleasure of spending time with in your most magical years. You are all so beautiful and lovely.

Contents

" In the midst of a luminous ocean, we stood almost blind.

—*Sir Jagadis Chandra Bose*

Introduction

If you read this first it will make the rest of the book a lot easier to understand. :)

How did I find myself writing and illustrating a book without knowing what I was doing and how I was going to do it? And why on earth did I find myself in this predicament? This question annoyed me for most of 2009 and started to plague me in 2010. It all began when I attended a writing workshop and, while there, became convinced that writing and illustrating a book was a *great* idea. Without further ado, I'd landed myself with a publishing deadline. During numerous stages of the book-hatching process, I found myself scrambling around, researching information here and there, leaping from one topic to another and generally looking like a hysterical chook in a flap.

With the gentle guidance and wisdom of a few friends and other creative individuals, it dawned on me that the only book I could possibly write was the one that was residing quietly within my own world. It had been sitting in here patiently waiting to be written for some time. I knew this because I'd been looking for a book just like it for some time. This book I had been looking for was short and sweet, and explained very clearly and simply the basics of the creative process: how it works, why it doesn't work sometimes, why it's important, and how to best access and encourage our individual creative expression in any of its myriad forms.

This is what I've set out to cover in the following pages. This book is meant to be an enjoyable foray into understanding more about your own unique creativity, what inspires you, and how to experience more of it in your daily life. More than anything, I don't want to overburden you with too much information or too many lengthy and wordy passages. Creativity rarely follows a linear path. Unlike words, pictures can express a multitude of ideas, feelings and emotions simultaneously.

I've 'drawn' the book as much as I can and written only as much as necessary. When reading this, I'd like you to feel like you're taking a little holiday, during which you'll learn some interesting and useful things while deriving joy and refreshment from the experience. Upon your return from your holiday, you will feel like you're even more aware of the unique gifts that you bring with you to this life. (I refer to your soul at various stages during this book. I have no religious intention here. You can use any word that sounds right for you, like your *truth*, your *authenticity*, or your *heart*. I'm referring to a part of the individual and collective human experience that discerns something that is a part of the self but greater than itself.)

I would often go in search of this book in the outer world, asking people if they knew of a book like the one that was already imprinted in my own heart. Eventually I stopped the incessant scrambling and let the creative process take its natural course. This led to the unfolding of *Your Inner Knowing: Unlocking the Secrets to Creative Success*. Luckily I was taken through this creative process by a most helpful and insightful little character called **YIK** …

Hello!
My name's YIK...

A word from YIK …

I guess you might know me as Your Intuition, Your Gut Feeling, Your Heart or Your Sixth Sense. Either way, it's all much the same thing and we do the same job. I like pictures, mainly because right now I am one! I often use pictures to communicate with you, as well as feelings, sounds, smells and intuition. And, of course, words; they're quite useful too.

The only reason I exist in the particular form you are looking at is because my copilot was having trouble writing this book. She likes pictures a lot, and the easiest way to get her to listen to me was to show up in one. This helped her get a grip on her Inner Knowing. Between the pair of us, we scribbled out a bunch of words and pictures to make up this book.

Everything in the following pages is about the creative process. The reason I feature so highly in the story is because your creativity is inextricably linked with me, Your Inner Knowing. So you can't find out about one without the other. Creativity is the expression of your heart and soul, and all three of us live here in your internal world.

We are forever trying to make contact with you, so we can assist you and brighten your life every day. But you're always so busy and stuck in the external world with its endless distractions that we don't get noticed all that much.

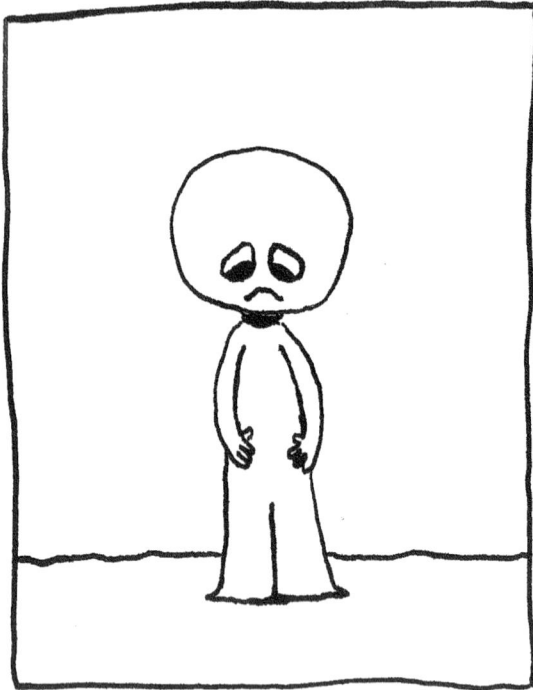

Which is sad. It's such a pity, because we're very useful and helpful.

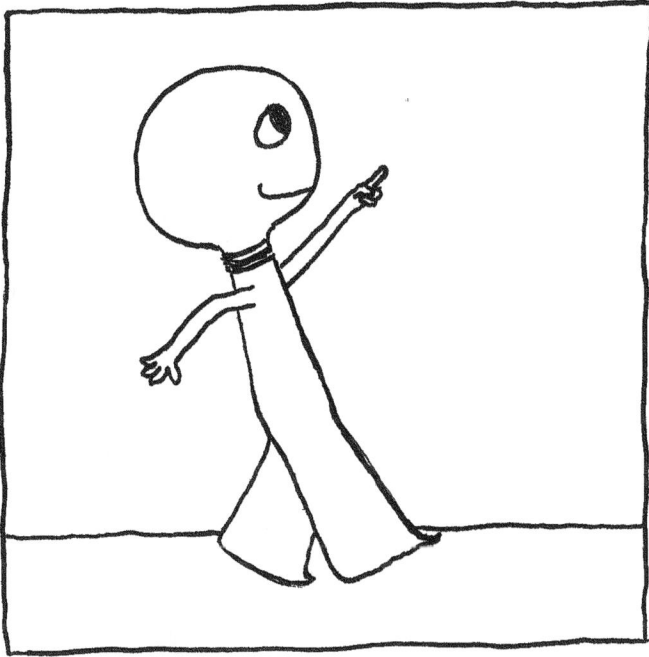

Anyway, here I am, finally in print so you can see and hear me very clearly. Without further ado, let's begin our grand adventure!

Part 1
Why creativity is so important

> ... creativity is the ability to devise or originate something new by thinking about it. This, in itself, is no mean feat considering whatever you're thinking about doesn't exist yet!
>
> —*Neroli Makim*

Chapter 1

Creativity: What is it?

Well, the place that seemed the most logical to seek out this information was *The Australian Oxford Dictionary*. Surely the publication that claims to define the English language should have some insight into the meaning of the word *creativity*. Now, if you can just follow through with this little exercise in understanding the essence of creativity, I think you'll be quite amazed and surprised by its findings.

Here's what the dictionary says about the word *creative*:

creative/adj   1.   imaginative or inventive

                          2.   creating or able to create creativity/n

So if you're creative, or you're expressing your creativity, you're able to create. You are imaginative and inventive. To really get to the bottom of what creativity is, we'll need to investigate the words *imaginative* and *inventive*.

The word *inventive*:

inventive/adj	1.	able or inclined to invent
	2.	original in devising
invent/v	1.	To create by thought, devise; originate (a new method, instrument, etc)

Please take note of those words: 'to create by thought'. So creativity is the ability to devise or originate something new by thinking about it. This, in itself, is no mean feat considering whatever you're thinking about doesn't exist yet!

And finally the word *imaginative*:

imaginative/adj	1.	Having or showing to a high degree the faculty of imagination/n
imagination/n	1.	A mental faculty forming images or concepts of external concepts not yet present to the senses

Ha! So there it is again! Here you are using some part of yourself that can form 'images or concepts of external objects' that don't even exist yet, are 'not yet present to the senses'!

The process of creativity appears to be the process of bringing things that are unknown and unseen by us (and the rest of the world) into our thoughts so we can observe and comprehend them. According to these dictionary definitions, *creativity* is our ability to create an image or concept of something, in thought form, that has not yet been conceived of and then bring it into the realm of our sensory perception.

Am I the only one getting excited about this? The dictionary's just told us we can create something out of nothing; that we have access to some world of the unknown that is beyond our senses; that we can gather insights and information and bring it into the world of sensory knowing. I would normally expect to hear this from some religion or dogma, or New Agey guru, but not the *Oxford Dictionary*! Woohoo! Who knew the good old *Oxford Dictionary* could be so philosophical?

I remember when I was at school and had to chant things in church about 'the creator of heaven and earth … of all that is seen and unseen', and I've heard plenty of self-help and New Age doctrines professing that we're the makers of our own reality. But here we have the dictionary, through definition, telling us that *we* are quite capable of creating the seen from the unseen. Obviously, if you look at the world around you it's easy to observe that we're a creative bunch. There's so much manmade stuff everywhere, and it all came from someone's creative inkling. But where does the inkling come from? It comes from the unseen, or the great unknown. The great unknown is a place beyond our sensory perception, where a part of our being can go, bring things back and make them into a form perceptible to our senses.

So, stay with me here, we're almost through and you're about to find out how YIK fits into it all. Everything we can perceive and sense in our outer, physical world has been created. At some time it must have been residing in this unseen and unknown world. Someone or something must have brought it from the unknown and unseen into the world we live in.

Which part of you has access to this infinite realm? Which part of you has the skill to traverse the unfathomable depths of the unknown, and bring forth insights and understanding to your outer world?

Your Inner Knowing, of course! Your Inner Knowing (YIK) is the only part of you that has the purity of intention required to bring the gifts of the soul to the surface. YIK's sole purpose in life is to bring you insights and wisdom from that pristine part of yourself that is love and truth, inspiring you to create to your heart's desire.

The only problem (and it's quite a big one) is that Your Inner Knowing speaks to you through your heart. Most of the time our hearts are being drowned out by the clutter and chaos of all the external influences that flood our lines of internal communication, along with being shouted down by the incessant chatter of our minds. How will you access Your Inner Knowing then? How will you bridge the gap between your conscious reality and your soul?

We'll answer these questions and more after exploring the definition of creativity a little more. In the following chapters I'll show you how the creative process actually works, and then how you can cultivate it in your own life, creating the bridge between Your Inner Knowing and your outer, conscious reality.

It's also worth noting here some of the ways Sir Ken Robinson defines creativity. After all, he's an internationally recognised leader in the development of creativity and innovation, a highly sought-after speaker on the topic, and has authored numerous books on the subject. I refer to him extensively throughout this book. I find him to be fabulously interesting, entertaining and insightful, so why not whack some Sir Ken in here for good measure?

Here are some of the ways Sir Ken describes creativity:

- An imaginative process with outcomes that are original and have value.

- Creativity impacts the public world.

- Being creative involves doing something; it is a process, not an event.

- Creativity takes place in a medium; that is, it is communicated to our senses through some material or activity.

- Creativity is not a purely personal process. Many creative processes draw from the ideas and stimulation of other people. Creativity flourishes in an atmosphere where original thinking and innovation are encouraged and stimulated.[2]

All of the above are perfect guides in helping define creativity. In this book, however, you will notice that I often advocate removing yourself from external stimuli to help nurture and cultivate your own creativity. I agree wholeheartedly with the statement that creativity is not a purely personal process, and it thrives on inspiration from others.

For the purpose of getting in touch with your own inner creative voice, if you don't already know your unique expression of creativity very well you'll need to spend some time in a private dialogue with your internal world. This will help you become clear about what you would really love to share with the world. We'll also look at why this is so important in the chapters on how creativity works and how to cultivate it.

And one last little afterthought before moving on (please insert bossy voice here!): I don't want to hear any of you saying or thinking 'I'm just not creative'. Nonsense! Saying 'I'm not creative' or 'I'm no good at creativity' is like saying 'I'm not breathing' or 'I'm no good at breathing'.

As we shall see in the next chapter, creativity is a natural, organic process that's an innate part of being human, just like breathing. If you're a living, breathing human, you are creative. Woohoo! How cool is that?

So now that's all cleared up, let's move onto the next chapter and find out how creativity works.

> A new idea is a light that illuminates things that simply had no form for us before the light fell on them and gave them meaning.

—*Sir Ken Robinson*

Chapter 2

Creativity: How does it work?

It's very simple really. Most things are. We're the ones that complicate them and make life difficult. The creative process is really just like the natural organic process of all life on this planet. It resembles breathing in that it's a constant movement of thoughts, ideas and consciousness from within and without. We've done a lot to distance ourselves from nature's ebb and flow, but that doesn't change the fact that we are inextricably linked to it. Our survival depends on it whether we like it or not. Let's take a look …

Imagine your creative idea or inkling is a seed. This seed is something that you may have collected in your travels (gathering ideas, insights and wisdom from both your inner and outer world) or it may have been given to you. Either way, you have this seed or creative inkling. If you want to develop it, you *must* plant the seed. That is, you must let it settle within your thoughts and give it some space to grow within your conscious mind.

NB (this is important): It's well documented that if you want a seed to grow into a strong and healthy plant, the first thing you need to do is plant it in rich, fertile soil. The same goes for your creative inkling. If you want it to grow into a strong and healthy creation, it must be planted in a mind that is conducive to growing great ideas into magnificent creations. If our bodies and minds are toxic, barren wastelands, we'll have a hard time creating anything substantial. There'll be a lot more on this in the chapters on cultivating your creativity.

Once planted, you'll need to nourish the seed. Your creative idea is housed in both your body and mind, so you'll need to feed and water your body well to facilitate the creative inkling's growth. You'll need to nourish the idea in your mind by giving it space in your thoughts so you can contemplate and reflect on it. What we put into our body and mind may not seem so important when it comes to our creativity but, as you will see, it plays a significant role.

Imagine feeding any other living thing, plant or animal with caffeine, sugar, chemicals and weird things masquerading as food. Would you expect a plant to grow from a tiny seed into a strong, healthy tree that bears delicious and beautiful fruit and flowers? Definitely not! Neither can you expect your body and mind to thrive creatively when it's undernourished and burdened with unhealthy things. I'll explore this further in the true food nude section on how to cultivate your creativity.

Continue to nurture your creative inkling, trusting all the while in its natural, organic, growing process. Think about it. When you plant a seed you don't need to poke around in the dirt and inspect the roots to see if it's growing yet. In fact, to do so would be detrimental to the seed's growth process. You just plant it and nurture it as needed, trusting that it will sprout out of the ground into a seedling. The same goes for your creative evolution: it will progress in a natural and organic process.

Just like an acorn knows to grow into an oak tree, your creative inkling will follow its own innate knowing towards complete expression, if you let it.

You don't need to prod around and over-analyse your creativity constantly. Just like digging around in the dirt and upsetting the seedling's roots, this can be detrimental to your embryonic creative inkling. Of course, investing your time and money in preparation, contemplation and education can assist in making a fertile habitat for your creative expression. This can be likened to preparing the soil. But if you're not careful, overdoing it can easily interfere with the mystery and magic of your intrinsic creative unfurling.

Hugh MacLeod, author, artist and advocate of rediscovering and expressing our creativity, warns against 'hiding behind pillars' instead of trusting in our own ability and working with what we've got. From his observations, people who must have the latest, most expensive tools and gadgets in order to express their creativity aren't being particularly creative at all. Instead of using their innate creative gifts and raw talent, he believes they're 'hiding behind pillars' (hiding behind their fancy gadgets) and 'there is no correlation between creativity and equipment ownership'.[3]

There are plenty of overeducated, underwhelming and frustrated creatives among us. Excessive analysis, education and preparation is an easy trap to fall into if you don't trust yourself and your innate creative ability. Not trusting in Your Inner Knowing and creative ability *will* stunt the growth of your creative expression and fulfilment, just as not trusting another person will stunt the growth of a relationship.

NB: The word 'creatives' is my own made-up word. I've been using it for some time because it seems like a perfectly good word that needs to exist in the English dictionary. 'Creatives' refers to any persons who are actively engaged in any creative process, so it's really just a fun way to refer to humans.

> Although there are always points where criticism is necessary, generative thinking has to be given time to flower. At the wrong point, it can kill an emerging idea.[4]

—*Sir Ken Robinson*

Finally! You rejoice to see the first shoots of your new creation making itself known to the world. This is a great time to share your budding creation with people you know will treat it with care. Your creation is still in its infancy, and it wouldn't be wise to put it under intense scrutiny and dissection by careless individuals at this stage.

As a newborn takes their first glimpse of the outer world, they are going to have a pretty severe experience of life on the outside if strangers are allowed to prod and analyse them. The newborn may not like it at all, compared to where they spent the last nine months. Their little baby cells and psyche might hold onto these impressions and let them shape how they view life.

In the same way that external influences shape a child's blueprint for life, your budding creativity also grows and evolves through these influences. Like a very impressionable, tiny child, your fragile creative expression is still learning about itself and its own strength, scope and abilities. If you don't trust in your creativity and let Your Inner Knowing shape its evolution, others will do so. When you let others become the directors of your creative expression, the wisdom and power that comes from learning to dance to the beat of your own heart is lost.

It's worth noting here that 'creativity is not a purely personal process. Many creative processes draw from the ideas and stimulation of other people'.[5] This is an enjoyable and vital element of the creative process. In fact, cross-pollination is a huge part of the creative process. Creativity thrives and evolves from this in the same way nature does.

From my own observations I believe it helps to work towards being quite grounded in your creative medium first; then other people can inspire you, without you becoming copies of them. Looking within is just as beneficial and vital to your creative process as looking without. I'll go into this further in a later chapter on cultivating your own creativity.

It's worth keeping in mind that if you don't have a strong connection to Your Inner Knowing and don't feel grounded in your own creative play, then it will be all too easy to dilute the clarity and beauty of your own heart and soul's song with someone else's. Continue to nourish and nurture your creativity with contemplation, conversation and taking action wherever necessary to keep it alive, healthy and growing.

At this point we need to look some more at the role of Your Inner Knowing and the magical mystery of the creative process. In my own creative endeavours, often the greatest triumph and achievement happens by 'accident', when I'm not pushing or forcing anything but just playing around. I've heard this is the case with numerous creatives in every imaginable field and discipline.

A great example of this can be found in Richard Feynman's story of how he came to win the Nobel Prize for physics. He decided he was just going to do things for the fun of it. By playing around with his observations without attaching any importance to them, in a very short time he worked out the things that would later win him the Nobel Prize for his work in quantum electrodynamics.[6]

When playing creatively, something amazing pops into the game that you would never in a million years have come up with all on your own when you're not forcing an agenda onto the process. It's also known as serendipity or chance. This is precisely the role of Your Inner Knowing: to bring these glimpses of brilliance – this insight and wisdom – to the surface of your conscious mind. Busily listening to what everyone else says and forcing an agenda on your creativity leaves no room for magnificent mistakes.

There's no space for Your Inner Knowing to join in the game. With no room for magnificent mistakes your creations will be devoid of input from the infinite mystery; from your heart and soul. We discover how this can have a devastating effect on your creative expression in the section on cultivating creativity.

It's still important to treat your creation with the love and attentiveness you would give to anything you value highly, even when it has found its own strength and momentum. This attention will not only help you define your creative gifts and abilities more clearly, it will also make you aware of your weaknesses. This is just as important as knowing your strengths.

People who are really successful in expressing their creativity know their weaknesses and find ways to turn them into strengths, or go around them by delegating or dumping whatever they can. Again, MacLeod's words are worth referencing: 'Picasso was a terrible colourist, Turner couldn't paint human beings worth a damn … Bob Dylan can't sing or play guitar.'[7] These creative limitations didn't stop any of these men from being amazing individuals. Each one left a powerful imprint of their unique soul's language in our collective consciousness.

During the various stages of writing this book I gave it to friends and family to read and critique for me. I've had the greatest help from people looking at my creative expression, showing me areas of weakness where the book didn't read clearly or fluently. They even told me when it sounded too bossy. It's hard to know your own weaknesses because you're so involved in the creative process. Our blindspots stop us from seeing things that others can spot easily from their perspective.

Having others help you to see where there is room for improvement or the need to rework some aspects of your creation is a vital and rewarding part of the creative process. But put your creativity out there for feedback only when you've reached a stage in the process where you're ready to take constructive criticism on board and really make it work for you. (Hurrah for clever permaculture goddesses with scientific minds, like Scarlett Patrick, who returned the manuscript to me within twenty-four hours with the most extraordinarily clear, concise and useful feedback on areas of weakness laid out in point form! Now that is an impressive example of the art of creative fine-tuning and pruning in action.)

Your Inner Knowing is not an accidental visitor. It will direct you to the people, places, events, experiences and inspiration you need to cultivate your unique blend of creative expression.

—*Neroli Makim*

At long last! Your creation is out there in full bloom for all to see. Not everyone will love it as you do. If it is your own, authentic, creative expression it will bring joy and fullness to your heart and give you something far more valuable than public accolade. You will have learned through your own experience to trust life, the creative process and your ability to create something from nothing. As far as recognition for your creativity goes, again MacLeod says it perfectly: 'It wasn't the format that made the art great. It was the fact that somehow while playing around with something new, suddenly they found they were able to put their entire selves into it … That's what people responded to. The humanity, not the form … Put your whole self into it, and you will find your true voice. Hold back and you won't. It's that simple.[8]

I love that. People will respond to your creative expression depending on how much of your heart and soul has gone into it. And it *is* that simple.

Remember how I said that it's devastating to your creative expression to leave out your heart and soul? Well, that's why it's so important! That's what touches others: the authentic voice of your heart and soul in your creation. The more your creation is watered down by other people's ideas and creativity, the less impact it has on others. The energy of your heart and soul is extremely powerful. If it's been dissipated by an overload of external influences it becomes dull, boring, repetitive and devoid of any real creativity. It's a bit like an education system that operates on rote learning and educates people to become good workers rather than creative thinkers.

Johann Wolfgang von Goethe, one of Germany's most famous philosophers and one of the most influential thinkers in Western culture, observed that there are successive rhythms of expansion and contraction in a plant's life cycle. This rhythm of expansion and contraction in a plant can be likened to the rhythm of breathing: in/out, contraction/expansion, inspire/expire. Your creative process follows a rhythm similar to a plant's life cycle.

Remember how I said that if you're breathing, you're creative? Your creativity involves both the receptive and active principals. Inspiration comes from the people and things around you. You literally take this inspiration into the greatest depths of your being and allow it to incubate within you.

A magical and alchemical melding happens between your own inner world and the outer world, bringing forth a new creation born of the two. Just like the rhythm of the breath, there is a moment between inspiration and expiration in which nothing is going in or coming out; there is a moment of stillness and silence. This is the place where the magic and mystery happens! This is the space you need to allow for Your Inner Knowing to manifest. It is here that your unique soul print (USP) is embedded into your creation.

Most people know the abbreviation USP as 'unique selling point'. Without a USP your business is lost, drowning in the sea of everyone else who is selling the same thing. As far as creativity is concerned, your unique soul print (USP) is the only thing that gives your creativity the power to make an impression on others. If you rush along and don't allow Your Inner Knowing to make a significant imprint on your creation, then it becomes a lot like a copy of what's already out there in the world. Your creativity won't look and feel interesting, or be insightful and fresh. It won't make a powerful impression on others.

> Plant the seeds. It's easy. It's fun.
> You know how to do it — you were
> born knowing how.
>
> —*Neroli Makim*

If you're wondering how to ensure it's your authentic expression, keep your creation protected from an overdose of external influence in its infancy. We'll explore some ways to get in touch with our Inner Knowing in the section on play and cultivating creativity.

Now, you might think this is where the story ends, but no. Not by a long shot. In fact, it's barely begun. This is where it gets *really* exciting! As with all natural cycles on Earth there is a birth, life and death phase. Often we humans don't deal well with the death phase of anything and try to hang on and keep things alive well past their time. But this is the real kicker in the game of life and creativity.

When the plant goes into a death or transition phase, it gifts you with the seeds to create new life. The same goes for your creativity. Once the blooming stage is over and the life cycle of your creativity is in transition, you have the opportunity to reap the seeds of your creation. These seeds can be gratitude, financial remuneration, social acknowledgement and new opportunities to express more of your creativity. Woohoo! This is *great*! Who knew death could be so wonderful and rewarding?

The following picture demonstrates the rewards of death and transition perfectly. From planting that one little seed, and nurturing that one little creative inkling, the universe can give you so much in return. Life won't do the work for you. Life gives you the seeds and supports your creative expression and evolution.

You must prove to be a worthy recipient of life's gifts. You need to use your creative ability wisely, *and* trust in yourself and life's natural cycles. Then you will get more … and more … and more … and *more* opportunity to experience and express your creative genius. If you never bother to plant those seeds you're carrying around inside yourself, expect to spend the rest of your life wondering why other people are so lucky/have all the fun/get all the opportunities, and so on ad infinitum.

And now a quick word on creativity, life and death. Nothing too heavy. When you think about it, life and all its creations thrive on death, or depend on something dying in order to live. Plants live on the dead and decaying material of other plants and animals. Animals, including people, live on other dead plants or animals. All of life and all creative works require some form of death in order to live; however, a lot of our creations require the death of many things in order to live.

I've had the privilege of learning more about this cycle of life and death/creation and destruction from Dr John Demartini. Dr Demartini is a human behavioural specialist who shares his insights with millions of people all over the world, almost every day of the year. In his work, he assists people in understanding the divine balance of life and death, creation and destruction, and to observe that one never happens without the other. Something must die in order for new life to occur.

Destruction and creation go hand in hand – that seems like a feasible enough law to grasp and work with. As players in the game of life, we get to decide how we go about creating and destroying. We can choose to destroy other things, besides Earth and its ecosystems, in order to express our creativity.

I think it's intriguing to see how we humans can create flourishing cohabitation, with Earth and its myriad life forms, rather than choose to destroy it in order for us to live.

If you want to observe the law of creation and destruction in action, take a look at the things happening in your life. You can observe that some businesses require the death of other businesses in order to thrive. Some relationships require the death or demise of other relationships in order to flourish. Most urban environments require the death of natural ecosystems in order to exist.

Right now, I'm killing the lawn in my garden so I can put garden beds in that space and grow vegetables. Right now, in my street a lot of old houses are being developed into high-density apartment blocks. Instead of the blocks in the street housing hundreds of billions of micro-organisms in the soil, plants, earthworms, bugs, insects, birds, possums, chooks and a few humans, they will house a lot of steel and concrete, a lot more humans and all the stuff we generally carry around to fill our spaces with. This is neither here nor there; it's just what happens in cities with their ever-increasing population density. But it shows clearly the law of life and death, creation and destruction in action. All the topsoil, with all the plants, organisms and micro-organisms living in and on it, die in order for us to go on living in our preferred style.

I mentioned at the beginning of the chapter how dependent we are on the earth and its ecosystems for our survival. Even though most of us know this in an intellectual sense, I don't think this knowledge really occurs for us on an experiential level because life in urban environments keeps us removed from this reality.

I'll end this chapter with an amazing observation from Jonas Salk, medical researcher and virologist, that brings this point home very clearly:

If all the insects were to disappear from the earth, within fifty years all of life on earth would end. If all human beings on earth disappeared from the earth, within fifty years all forms of life would flourish[9]

—*Jonas Salk*

Part 2
Creative catalysts

> I love this game; playing is my inspiration. When I look in the eyes of those around me, it's clear that we've come here for the same thing. Let's play!
>
> —*Neroli Makim*

Chapter 3

Let's play!

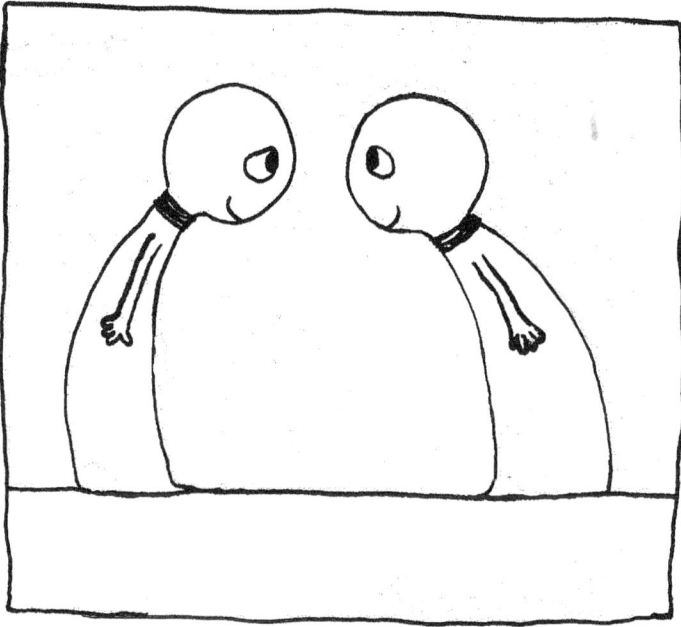

This section is solely devoted to the art of playing. Without play, creativity doesn't exist. End of story. But just in case that rock-solid argument doesn't convince you, Dr Stuart Brown just might. He's a medical doctor, psychiatrist, clinical researcher and published author who has spent his entire career studying the nature of play in humans. In his book *Play*, which covers his life's work to date, he states: 'Play lies at the core of creativity and innovation. Authentic play comes from deep down inside of us … it emerges from the imaginative force within.'[10]

Remember that Your Inner Knowing speaks to you through your heart. There can be a problem sometimes when the transmission is shut down between Your Inner Knowing, your heart and your conscious mind. Dr Bowen White, a pioneer in stress medicine, a physician, speaker and author, says: 'Play opens your heart, and then you can see what's inside.'[11]

But back to Dr Stuart Brown. Play is the language YIK uses to convey messages from the unknown to your conscious mind. Play is the language in which our creative genius speaks most fluently to us. Dr Stuart Brown states that the essence of play is freedom. Studies have shown that the biggest hindrance to creativity is a lack of freedom and autonomy, so the vital ingredient for both play and creativity is the same.

Dr Brown has described seven fundamental elements that characterise authentic play. Let's take a look at these seven elements and see how they're deeply ingrained in the creative process.

'Play is apparently purposeless, done for it's own sake. It doesn't help in getting money or food, it doesn't have a [recognised] survival value.'

I added the word 'recognised' to Dr Brown's quote because I'm sure play has a very significant survival value for humans, as you will see when I discuss what led him to begin studying play behaviour in humans in the first place.

Now, why is purposelessness (a very hard word to say, a real physical challenge – try repeating it three times) so important to our creative process?

> You can discover more about a person in an hour of play than in a year of conversation.

—*Plato*

Purposeless play is connected to improvisational potential. In order to think creatively, we need to be able to think holistically. We need to use our ability to take as many disparate themes and concepts as possible and draw insights from them. This is what happens in purposeless play. Because of the inherently purposeless nature of authentic play, we naturally slip into a holistic mind set.

The biggest hindrance to accessing our creative or holistic thinking ability is to be intently focused on getting some outcome, figuring something out, or under stress and pressure to produce a result. This is the opposite of purposeless play, and we become locked in narrow, linear thinking. Purposeless play does not and cannot happen by consciously thinking about it. We have to literally be playing just for the fun of it, allowing it to happen naturally, to become absorbed in our playful activity.

We can begin a play activity with the intention of gathering some insights about a problem we're working on, but consciously thinking about the problem has to be left at the doorway in order for us to access the kind of thinking needed to find our answers. That's the first major connection between play and accessing our creativity.

'Play is voluntary, not obligatory or a required duty.'

Put another way, freedom and autonomy are vital to the creative process. Basically, both play and creativity don't exist without freedom and autonomy. So if we're playing authentically we're in a very fertile creative space, because we're engaged in something that's completely voluntary. We cannot be forced to play and we cannot be forced to be creative, by ourselves or anyone else. The very act of someone imposing their will or any kind of restraint (including our own self-inflicted restraints) on us immediately closes down our ability to play authentically or think holistically/creatively.

You will hear me consistently reiterate that we need to allow the play and creative process to happen naturally, because it *must*; it's the only way it works. It can't be contrived or forced.

We are naturally playful and creative beings; we're born like this. When we were kids we just did it, and we still do if we let ourselves; we inherently know how to be playful and creative.

'Play = inherent attraction, it's fun and it makes us feel good. Play is exciting and it's a cure for boredom.'

Dr Brown says that nothing lights up the brain like play, referring to the increased neural connections being made when we're engaged in playing. The experience of fun and excitement in play puts us in a heightened state of mental and physical arousal (increased neural connections), which increases our creative thinking.

Visualise the massive influx of neural connections taking place in the brain during play. Now translate that to our ability to take abstract themes and concepts and connect them to come up with creative and innovative solutions to problems. It's a weird thing to comprehend, but, literally, the more neural connections we generate through play the more we're able to make the connections needed for creative and innovative thinking.

'Play gives us a sense of freedom from time; when we're fully engaged in play, we lose track of time.'

Ha! There it is again, the f-word! In relation to play and creativity, it just keeps coming up again and again, doesn't it? Most of us experience time as a very linear, sequential process. Remember what we've said about linear and sequential processes as far as creativity is concerned? Linear and sequential is a killer when it comes to creativity. Certainly we love process; as mentioned before, creativity is a process, not an event. But the creative process thrives on a multilevel, holistic, and even cyclical approach.

Linear and sequential constraints of time totally mess with play and creativity if we allow these constraints to dictate our creative brainstorming. This is, understandably, a big issue we all face. We live in a world where we're constantly under time constraints, and we have to deal with that, but we can and do, every day.

The trick is to ensure you give yourself the time out needed in any given moment or day to recharge and refresh your creative batteries. Ensure that when you do give yourself this time out, you do whatever you need to get into a play state where you become totally absorbed and don't clock-watch.

Of course, sometimes it isn't possible to leap away from our work and immerse ourselves in play, but I do this whenever I can if the need arises. Dr Brown states that 'play is a catalyst ... enlivening everything else ... and making us more productive and happier in everything we do'. So when we do give ourselves that time out to engage in whatever form of authentic play we need to do to get into our zone, it can be enormously beneficial for our work and our overall wellbeing.

'Play gives us a diminished consciousness of self. We stop thinking or caring about what others think. We are fully in the moment, in the flow, or the zone.'

Having a diminished consciousness of self is a massive part of being successful with our creative and innovative thinking. Researchers have done studies proving that people will knowingly give incorrect responses to questions if they think being right will set them apart from the group or make them appear different.

What has this got to do with creativity and play? It has a lot to do with a diminished consciousness of self and caring what others think.

If we, as humans, are so wired to be concerned about fitting into a group that we will knowingly give incorrect answers just to ensure we belong or fit in, then finding a way to trip this wiring is vital to our creative abilities. We can (and will) stifle our creative insights if we're concerned about what others might say or think about them; in other words, if we're sensitive to external judgment or criticism (and we are).

Play is our tripwire. As Dr Brown has stated, in authentic play we stop caring about what others think and we lose our sense of self-consciousness.

Ask any creative if they're concerned about what someone thinks of their work. How badly does it mess with their creative process? Ask yourself this same question in relation to anything you're working on. If you care too much about what others think, does it diminish your ability to do it well?

Being able to immerse yourself deeply in any activity so external influence or approval doesn't interfere with our creative process is vital to your success.

It's through play that we can find the path to this lack of self-consciousness. After all, we're just playing, right? It's no big deal, it's a game and we don't place the same expectations on ourselves when we're playing, and neither do others. Play gives us the out we need to shake off the expectations of ourselves and other people, and open up to our creative potential.

'Play allows for improvisational potential. We aren't locked into rigid ways of thinking or doing things. We are open to serendipity or chance ... we stumble upon new behaviors, thoughts, strategies, movements, or ways of being. We see things in a different way and have fresh insights ... You never know what's going to happen when you play.'

I mentioned earlier that purposeless play was connected to improvisational potential. Obviously, our ability to improvise is an essential part of creativity and innovation. Improvisation is what takes us from a known to an unknown path. Improvisation is how we make a map to navigate uncharted territory.

When we play, we allow ourselves to go off on tangents, to entertain unusual ideas or methods, and we allow ourselves to slip between what we know (or think we know) and the unknown. The same thing happens in our creative process.

Both play and creativity require improvisational potential in order to flourish. Without it the game stops, and so does the creative process. Play is an important ally for accessing our creativity and improvisational potential because in a play state we're more open to it.

The purposeless element of play allows us to recognise and respond to the things that might normally slip by unnoticed or unexplored if we were focused purely on an outcome. Through purposeless play we let ourselves pick up seemingly random elements, and improvisation is the skill we use to makes sense of these elements. We then engage our creativity to express the discoveries of our improvisational play.

'Play involves continuation desire, we want to keep doing it, the pleasure of the experience drives this desire.'

This aspect of play relates to fine-tuning our creative gifts more than anything else. Continuation desire helps us achieve mastery, which is an innate human psychological need. In his book *Drive*, Dan Pink states that humans have three innate psychological needs: autonomy, mastery (competence) and connection. Continuation desire is connected to fulfilling our need for mastery, or competence.

I read that anyone who has achieved mastery has spent at least ten thousand hours practising. I don't think we're going to achieve mastery in anything that requires that much practice unless we really love doing it. And what was that about play? Oh, wow! We want to keep doing it and the pleasure of the experience drives this desire? Cool! Then I guess that's the missing link to how we achieve mastery in our lives.

If we connect our work with play, we experience continuation desire and are more likely to put in the hours of dedication needed to attain a level of mastery.

This last aspect of play in relation to our creativity really leads into another whole world of exploration, and that is Sir Ken Robinson's work on finding our element. Basically, one of the things that quantifies finding my element for me is that I want to keep coming back to it again and again.

In other words, there is a strong continuation desire in my element; my element, which is my unique form of creative expression, is also a form of play for me. I would never put in the hours I do if I didn't love what I'm doing. My creative expression has to be a form of play for me in order to achieve any degree of mastery. And I'll bet this is the same for anyone who has accomplished any level of mastery in their lives.

Now you can see how play is integral to your creative process, and how your preferred style of play shifts you into the alternate space you need to be in to access your creativity.

So why don't we hear these messages clearly? Why aren't we all living creatively fulfilled lives and having great fun playing the game of life?

It seems we don't always give play the time or energy it deserves in our lives. In response to me talking about the importance of play and creativity, I often hear people say, 'Well, we're not kids anymore. We've got responsibilities. We've got to work and pay the rent/mortgage and put food on the table.' I agree, but some people have mastered the art of being paid to play. It's entirely possible that the work you're engaged in could be a form of play for you.

When I look in the faces of the people in the city streets, I very rarely see the vibrant aliveness apparent in the faces of people engaged in their favourite style of play.

All too often, while we're stressing ourselves 'making our living' we're also in the process of 'making our dying', or to put it more accurately, destroying our wellbeing. If the laws of creativity state that you cannot have creation without destruction, then it's best not to destroy your health and wellbeing. The end game of destroying your health and wellbeing is often being six feet under or catatonic from either drugs or depression.

Dr Brown goes on to say that 'the opposite of work isn't play, it's depression'.'[12] Ideally we will find work we love so that it's like being paid to play anyway. Some people have mastered this, and when you have mastered being paid to play, you have mastered a fairly major aspect of your life.

For the time being, many of us need to balance work that pays the bills and also allows some of our play personality to shine, as well as playing in our spare time. If you're not currently getting paid to play, then making time for both work and play in life is absolutely vital to your mental, emotional, social, spiritual and physical health.

Playing for life

To demonstrate just how important play is, it's worth knowing what led Dr Brown to begin studying play in humans. As a young assistant professor in psychiatry, he was thrust into the role of leading an investigative team of specialists to uncover why Charles Whitman committed a mass murder–suicide at Baylor College of Medicine, where Dr Brown worked. When each of the committee members investigating the cause of Whitman's homicidal breakdown assembled to share their findings, they had reached a unanimous conclusion: a lifelong lack of play!

A key factor leading to Whitman's psychopathology was the absence of fundamental life skills from this lack of play.[13] This is obviously an extreme case demonstrating the necessity of play for our health, but it clearly shows how play is a vital component in our healthy development and evolution.

Robert Fagen is the world's foremost expert on why animals play. According to Fagen, 'in a world continuously presenting unique challenges and ambiguity, play prepares animals (that means us too) for an evolving planet'.[14]

Robert Fagen's findings are supported by Sir Ken Robinson. Sir Ken speaks about the need for creativity to be nurtured and encouraged in children and adults. Creativity has to be actively sought out and championed in every individual in order for us to navigate the extraordinary challenges of our rapidly changing planet. Life on Earth, it seems, requires an abundance of both play and creativity if we're to continue to flourish and thrive.

So what are the reasons we aren't all engaged in joyful play and living a life of abundant creativity? Our Inner Knowing speaks to us through our hearts in the language of play. If we're not in contact with our Inner Knowing then the transmission lines are down.

We've heard that play opens the heart. What if we're all grown up; bogged down in the responsibilities of life and have forgotten about playing? How often do we engage in a preverbal, emotionally inspired feeling and intuitive experience? That's called playing. If your heart is closed, how do you open it? Luckily, you're about to discover some of the easiest and most enjoyable ways to make that connection.

While researching the science of play and its biological and evolutionary function, Dr Brown spent time learning from Robert Fagen's extensive studies into animal play.

One of the easiest ways to reconnect with your playful side and open your heart is to get moving! Although Dr Brown has found that physical movement is a surefire way to get people to reconnect with their inner play compass, there are myriad ways to get moving. You can move physically, emotionally, mentally and spiritually. The next chapter on play personalities will help you discover which kind of movement opens your heart most effectively.

Chapter 4

Ways we play

During decades of research and hundreds of case studies, Dr Brown has found that there are eight dominant styles of playing, and people generally have a preference for certain ways of playing over others. He called these 'play personalities'. They can help you connect with your favourite way to play. None of these play personalities are fixed. We can move through all of them in different situations, but generally each of us will find the most joy in one or two dominant modes of play.[16]

By familiarising yourself with these personalities, you will find out where and how to make the connection with the type of play that holds the keys to opening your heart and unleashing your creative genius. Understanding your preferred ways to play is an integral part of connecting with your own style of creativity. Sir Ken explains this perfectly when he says: 'Too often people conclude they're not creative when in truth, they may not have found how they are creative. By not finding their medium, they haven't found themselves.'[17]

Finding your medium is finding the kind of play that connects you to your unique style of creativity, or your creative character.

At the end of each play personality, there are a series of questions to ask yourself to help find out which play personalities you are most compatible with. When you look at the combinations of the play personalities you associate with most, then you can see what your creative character looks like. In the next chapter there is a quiz that helps you see which are your favourite play personalities. If you go to my website (www.yourcreativesuccess.com) you can fill out this same quiz and I'll email you a picture of your play personality.

The best way to determine your dominant play personality is to think about the activities that bring you into an experience of any or all of the following:

- You become less self-conscious and lose track of time because you're so immersed in the activity.

- It's something you do just for the fun of it, and you do it voluntarily.

- It makes you feel good and relieves boredom, and you're open to chance and serendipity (Your Inner Knowing) dropping into the activity and adding an unexpected element to it that brings new insights and ideas.

- Lastly, it's something you want to do again and again. It's something that gives you so much joy, pleasure and fulfilment that you come back to the activity or an improvised version of it whenever you can.[18]

These are all aspects of play that people will experience in some way when immersed in their favourite activities.

Movement fills an empty heart.

—Robert Fagen

The joker

A great friend of mine, Anna Lisa, is renowned for her repertoire of jokes and her uncanny ability to have people in stitches with her cheeky sense of humour. She has an extraordinary memory that easily recalls an endless supply of jokes. I never see her without being regaled with a few of the latest and finest. This gift is not only entertaining for her friends and family, but extremely useful in her work.

Anna and her husband Luca own a business that produces, imports and exports fine foods nationally and internationally. On a daily basis, Anna Lisa needs to communicate with people all over the world from all walks of life, sometimes in highly stressful situations. Besides dealing deftly with the occasional furious chef wielding a razor-sharp kitchen knife, or a highly agitated customer wondering if his shipment of olive oil has arrived, Anna Lisa's joker makes the environment in the office light and playful, which keeps things humming along in easy and difficult times.

Think about your life at home or work, or when you were in school:

Do you (or did you) love to play the class clown or prankster?

Are you the life of the party, always cracking people up with funny stories or jokes?

Even if you just love to go about quietly and make people smile or giggle, then the joker may be one of your most favoured play personalities.

The most basic and extreme player throughout history is the joker. A joker's play always revolves around some kind of nonsense. Parents make infants laugh by making silly sounds, blowing raspberries, and generally being foolish. Later, the class clown finds social acceptance by making other people laugh. Adult jokers carry on that social strategy.[19]

—*Dr Stuart Brown*

The kinaesthete

Over the years I've engaged in various physical activities, including horse riding, hockey, netball, swimming, running, yoga, Brazilian jui jitsu and capoeira. I was never a great sportsperson, even though I liked competition because it sometimes pushed me to train a bit harder. I really just loved testing my body to see what it could do. While it can be excruciating to be in a contorted Bikram Yoga posture in a room heated to thirty-seven degrees, it's great fun for me to see just what my body is capable of, and how much that changes with practice.

I experiment with different cleanses and fasts. This detoxifies my body, but I'm equally interested in testing it to see what happens and how it responds.

During school, I spent many lessons staring out classroom windows. I was desperate to be outside, playing and moving. Having to sit still in a room most of the day was torturous, except when I was in a class I liked. Most of these did not involve sitting still and listening to words. I loved any subject that involved active engagement: physical education, art and drama. I even enjoyed biology because I was able to relate it to the body and physical movement more so than the other sciences. (There was just one subject that didn't quite fit into the kinaesthete's preferred way to learn but I'll get to that later.)

Are you someone who needs to move in order to think?

Do you feel the most inspired and come up with your best ideas when you're exercising or engaged in some kind of physical movement?

When you were at school, did sitting at a desk listening to someone speak seem like an impossible task?

Were there other subjects that didn't involve sitting and listening that held your attention better?

If your answer to these questions was yes, then the kinaesthete is most likely one of your preferred play personalities.

Kinaesthetes are people who like to move, who, in the words of Sir Ken Robinson, 'need to move in order to think'. This category includes athletes, but also others who find themselves happiest moving as part of dance, swimming or walking. Kinaesthetes naturally want to push their bodies and feel the result. They may be those who play football, do yoga, dance, jump rope, or anything that physically moves their bodies. While kinaesthetes may play games, competition is not the main focus: it is only the forum for engaging in their favourite activity.[19]

—*Dr Stuart Brown*

The explorer

I've enjoyed exploring mostly in the manner of a personal inquiry into the way I work. It's fun to explore how I navigate the world, people and life, and how others do the same. This has led me to complete a four-year Diploma in Body Centred Psychotherapy, practise various kinds of meditation, including moving meditation (yoga) and still meditation (Vipassana). I've also attended numerous other courses in self-education and personal development. I inherited this interest in exploration from my father. He thrives on living on the land and examining how to create regenerative ecosystems, facilitating an even greater biodiversity in the natural habitat. This puts him, and his fellow explorers, at the real frontiers of maintaining and restoring Earth's clean and healthy food, air and water supply.

Have you loved to travel? This could involve physically going to new places and experiencing different cultures.

Have you loved to explore? This could be exploring through trying new types of food, exploring the many facets of the human psyche, or discovering new ways of communicating and creating. People who are at the frontiers of internet technology can be great examples of explorers.

If you love to explore and experience new things in any manner, then the explorer play personality could be one of the ways you love to engage in playing.

Each of us started our lives by exploring the world around us. Some people never lose their enthusiasm for it. Exploration becomes their preferred avenue into the alternate universe of play — their way of remaining creative and provoking the imagination. Think Richard Branson or Jane Goodall. Exploring can be physical – literally going to new places. Alternatively, it can be emotional – searching for a new feeling or deepening of the familiar; through music, movement, flirtation. It can be mental: researching a new subject or discovering new experiences and points of view while remaining in your armchair.[21]

—Dr Stuart Brown

The competitor

My experience of playing as a competitor is that it is usually short lived. I love competition to push me to get better at whatever I'm doing, galvanising me into action, but competing to win and be the best at something doesn't seem to keep my attention in the long term. I seem to fizzle out and lose interest long before becoming the world champion at anything. I do, however, have a very interesting story about two world-class competitors, in a gold-medal match, at the 2000 Olympic Games.

Kerri Pottharst and Natalie Cook were playing Brazil in the final match of the women's beach volleyball. Things just weren't going right for them. During a break, Dawn Fraser, Australia's greatest Olympian, a multi-Olympic medal winner who broke and held forty-one world records, approached them and said, 'You girls aren't having fun anymore. You need to enjoy yourselves, go out there to play and have fun, and have a great time!' That marked the turning point for the game. From that moment on, they got back into their winning rhythm and came from behind to beat the Brazilians in straight sets.

So, even if your play personality is the competitor, and you're a brilliant competitor, playing and having fun while you're at it is a key ingredient you need to win!

Do you have a strong competitive streak? Do you love to play to win?

Are you inclined like to keep score at whatever it is you're doing, whether it's a game of tennis, Nintendo or Scrabble?

Do you compete to earn the most money or maintain the most senior position in your work or social circle?

Do you find yourself competing with your partner to make the best pancakes?

If any kind of activity can become an opportunity for you to score points or compete to win, then the competitor play personality is going to be one of your favourites.

The competitor is a person who breaks through into the euphoria and creativity of play by enjoying a competitive game, with specific rules, and enjoys playing to win. He's the terminator. She's the dominator. The competitor loves fighting to be number 1. If games and keeping score are your thing, this may be your primary play personality. The games can be solitary or social – either a solitary video game or a team game like basketball – and they may be actively participated in or observed as a fan. Competitors make themselves known in social groups, where the fun comes from being the top person in the group, or in the business, in which money or perks service to keep the score.[22]

—Dr Stuart Brown

The director

I remember having the opportunity to sit in on the rushes of a film being produced by Uberto Pasolini, producer of the Oscar-winning film *The Full Monty*. Reviewing rushes takes place at the end of the day's filming, when the producer, director and other key creatives look over the shots and decide what works. It was late at night. Uberto and his co-workers were exhausted. This didn't stop him striding around the room, joyfully wielding a funny little net on a stick, like a tiny fishing net. It reminded me of a conductor leading an orchestra. Uberto looked wide awake, absolutely thriving in the play personality of the director.

In the past I've revelled in my role as host and key orchestrator. I used to organise numerous parties and gatherings and loved playing the director. When I played Capoeira, I organised a group that met in the park every Sunday to play and practise our moves; just hanging out and enjoying the afternoon as it hummed slowly into evening.

My mother has always been a great organiser of parties; she couldn't keep them low key if she tried! Even though we lived on a cattle station 160 kilometres from the nearest town and twelve kilometres from the nearest neighbours, Mum's parties and gatherings were grand affairs, complete with mouthwatering food and fine wine, and dancing or cricket on the tennis court beneath lights buzzing with kamikaze moths. To this day she still organises big family gatherings regularly. It's near impossible to try to arrange something on her behalf. She can't help but try to get involved and start twiddling away with the organising.

Are you a great party organiser? Being the instigator of social gatherings, whether at home or out on the town, is the director's realm of play and expertise. Or do you work in, or run a business that involves organising events and functions? Do you always find yourself taking on the role of being the go-to person in work, family or social situations that involves orchestrating meetings and events or developing agendas or managing groups of people?

If you like to be in charge and run the show, then it's safe to say you love to play the director, but no doubt you'll have some competitors around who are keeping score and trying to be number one!

Directors enjoy planning and executing scenes and events. Though many are unconscious of their motives and style of operating, they love the power, even when they are playing in the B-movie league. They are born organizers. At their best, they are party givers, the instigators of great excursions to the beach, the dynamic centre of the social world. All the world's a stage, and the rest of us are only players in the director's game. Good examples in this category are Barefoot Contessa chef Ina Garten and Oprah Winfrey.[23]

—*Dr Stuart Brown*

The collector

Keith Gardner is a man on a mission when it comes to collecting. Many years ago he decided he'd like to keep a few tropical fish. A few fish in one small tank turned into a few more fish, then a bigger tank … more fish … then two more tanks. Finally, three huge tanks with reinforced steel stands later, he thought he might move on to chickens! Nowadays, Keith keeps hundreds of rare, heritage-breed chickens. He breeds and sells them to all kinds of people, including the Prince of Wales. Keith's prized birds lay eggs that are sought after by chicken enthusiasts all over Europe. He doesn't collect or breed these birds in a competitive manner; he just does it because he loves it and can't help but become fastidiously involved in the collecting process.

Collecting can take many forms. It can be the collection of objects, experiences and memories, or perhaps you even like to collect data. Trainspotters are a prime example of data collectors. This kind of collector methodically notes down, collects and shares information about trains and their travel times. Collections come in many forms: recipes, tea cups, garden gnomes, wine, movie tickets, postcards, music, trips to the theatre … the list is endless. Let's just say: if it exists, you can most probably collect it

Is there an activity that you find irresistible that involves collecting of some kind? Is there a room in your house that has a collection of some kind filling the shelves and cupboards, or even spilling into the garage or basement?

Do you find yourself building a collection of information or data in which you spend time joyously noting down and collating your findings?

Is there an activity you love to engage in and keep a meticulous diary of every outing or experience?

Do you engage in some activity that involves collecting things or experiences and then sharing them with other enthusiasts?

All of these are aspects of the collector play personality. If you're smiling and nodding your head in recognition of any of these traits in yourself, then this has to be one of your favourite ways to play.

What good is a world of random objects? The thrill of play for the collector is to have and to hold the most, the best, the most interesting collection of objects or experiences. Coins, toy trains, antiques, plastic purses, wine, shoes, ties, video clips of race car crashes, or pieces of crashed cards themselves, anything and everything is fair game for the collector. One person I know travels the world to see solar eclipses – which might seem like the action of an explorer, except that he has to see every single one and methodically collects evidence of each eclipse. Collectors may enjoy collecting as a solitary activity, or they may find it the focus of an intense social connection with others who have similar obsessions.[24]

—Dr Stuart Brown

The artist/creator

This category has to be one of my major play personalities. After all, I'm writing a book about creativity. I've got a degree in fine art, and I've created artworks in drawing, painting, fibre sculpture, ceramic sculpture, bronze sculpture, photography and wearable art. My art has been shown in exhibitions and has been purchased for private and public collections nationally and internationally. For the most part, however, I engage in playing creatively for my own enjoyment and pleasure. Sometimes others like it too. :)

These days, I'm completely immersed in gardening as one of my major creative outlets. It keeps annoying me that I've got strawberry seedlings that need to be planted while I'm in here writing! From my experience as an artist creating in various mediums, I've come to be all the more inspired by the beauty, magnificence and perfection in nature. Looking at the way the sunlight plays on leaves and imagining how hard it is to capture that in a painting perplexes me. Trying to translate the golden glow of sunrise or sunset onto a canvas is equally challenging.

Even though I love the beauty of many art forms, there is something magical and alchemical in creating with the living earth that far surpasses anything I paint, draw or sculpt. When I look upon an artwork I've just completed, I'll often stare at it, mesmerised. It's as though I'm staring at some part of myself that's come from someplace deep within my soul. When I'm playing in the garden, co-creating with the earth and all the living organisms on it and in it, I get to experience more than just a visual reflection of my soul in my creativity.

Can you get lost for hours just twiddling with something and seeing what you can do with it or make from it? Are you someone who loves to experiment and play with things and doesn't really care if it works or not? Do you just love the process of playing around and seeing what happens? Do you thrive on making something – anything – from whatever is available to you at the time? Do you love the sense of timelessness that comes from being immersed in creativity, as much, and maybe even more so than getting to the finished product?

If you recognise any of these attributes in yourself, then the artist/creator play personality is sure to be one of your favourite modes of play.

For the artist/creator, joy is found is making things. Painting,
print-making, woodworking, pottery and sculpture are well-
known activities of artists/creators, but furniture making,
knitting, sewing and gardening are also in their purview.
Artists/creators may end up showing their creations to the
world and even selling them for millions, or may never show
anyone what they make. The point is to make something – to
make something beautiful, something functional, something
goofy. Or just to make something work – the artist/creator
may be someone who enjoys taking apart a pump, replacing
broken parts, cleaning it and putting it back together a shiny,
perfectly working mechanism; in effect, making it anew.[25]

—Dr Stuart Brown

The storyteller

Children are often the most amazing storytellers; they have such wild and free imaginations, engaging so easily in imaginative play. I've often sat and listened quietly to the make-believe stories of children. They ramble on uninhibited, telling extraordinary tales that keep them immersed in their play for hours. A great example of a fantastic and delightful child storyteller is 'Miss Capucine'. The extraordinary and hilarious tales of adventure and espionage the tiny Miss Capucine spins have to be listened to in order to get the full impact. If ever you'd like to see a storyteller with the imagination and creativity of a genius, you can find 'Miss Capucine – Once Upon a Time' on YouTube (www.youtube.com) or Vimeo (vimeo.com).

This is where the other subject I loved to be involved in at school – English – comes into the picture. I loved it because it allowed me to get lost in another of my favourite realms: the world of stories. While a lot of kids hated being given chapters of novels to read for homework, I loved it, and I happily read in my spare time anyway. In my last two years of primary school and early years of high school, I didn't have many friends or strong connections to any of my fellow students and my social life wasn't exactly booming. This caused me to spend even more time than before buried in books. I swapped boredom and loneliness for the fantasy worlds in the stories.

I would never wish to exchange my experience of those years for anything. The depth and richness of being immersed in the world of story still delights and surprises me to this day. I remember the times of living in the dreams, adventures and fantasies of stories with great fondness.

Growing up on an isolated cattle station, we didn't have a lot of the things most people take for granted. We didn't have electricity until 1986 and we had no television or telephone until 1990. When I wasn't outside actively engaged in my favourite kinaesthete or artist/creator modes of play, I would curl up in a big chair and lose myself in fantastic adventures and faraway lands. I was so blessed to have some of the most amazing stories to lose myself in.

Somehow, in our dingy little bookshelf that comprised the library, there were some big, heavy, hardcover books of folklore and fairytales from all around the world. In my imagination I could travel to places with witches, dragons,

knights, maidens, and faraway lands. As a young child I soaked up the stories and images of many exotic and intriguing cultures from all over the world. It was almost as if I'd actually been there, even though I was living in one of the most remote and isolated places in Australia. The true power and magic of story is often beyond our comprehension, but if you think about it a little you can see how powerful it is.

JK Rowling's success with the Harry Potter books exemplifies the power of myth and story. The Harry Potter books have been translated into sixty-five languages and the last four have set records as the fastest-selling books in history. The Harry Potter brand is estimated at a net worth of US$15 billion. When she wrote her first book, JK Rowling was a single mother on a pension; now she is ranked as one of the most powerful celebrities in the world.

All of these things are really just ways to measure the value of one woman's creative expression. The records, accolades and financial rewards show how much those stories have touched the hearts and minds of readers, and the impact of story in our lives.

Are you involved in any professional or recreational activities that involve performing or telling stories? Do you love to get lost in your own daydreams and imagination?

When you are in social situations, do you find yourself telling stories with such a natural ease and flair that you captivate your audience completely?

When you go to the movies, theatre or sports matches, or watch DVDs, do you become so immersed in the experience that you feel like you become part of it? Can you lose track of the time and everything else that's going on when immersed in these activities?

The storyteller play personality is going to be one of your favourite play styles if any of these characteristics sound familiar.

For the storyteller, the imagination is the key to the kingdom of play. Storytellers are, of course, novelists, playwrights, cartoonists and great screenwriters, but they are also those whose greatest joy is reading those novels and watching those movies, people who make themselves part of the story. Performers of all sorts are storytellers, creating an imaginative world through dance, acting, magic tricks and lectures. Because the realm of the storyteller is the imagination, they can bring play to almost any activity. They may be playing a recreational game of tennis, but in their mind, each point is part of an exciting drama. in contrast to the competitor, the storyteller's main point of the game is to have an exciting match. Even cooking macaroni and cheese can be transformed through imagination into a worldwide telecast celebrity cook-off.[26]

—*Dr Stuart Brown*

The inventor

The inventor is not one of Dr Brown's play personalities – although it infiltrates many of them – yet I'm drawn to discuss it individually with you anyway. It feels to me that another way to describe the artist/creator play personality would be as the inventor. Explorers often remind me of inventors as well.

Both my parents are good examples of creatives who are also inventors. My father invented numerous things out of necessity, including a set of gates that could trap wild cattle that lived in a forest and could not be mustered by any normal means. My mother is a genius of invention in the kitchen, throwing together all manner of foods and flavours, much like a mad alchemist in full swing.

I've inherited a love of food and cooking from my mother, as well as a lack of inhibition about throwing anything together and seeing what happens. Often, this can end disastrously! I'm completely unable to follow a recipe without heading off on my own little diversions and adding random elements here and guessing things there. I recently combined some recipes for pumpkin scones and cornbread to make 'pumpkin scorn bread'. I've reworked my great-grandmother's chocolate self-saucing pudding recipe so many times it's absurd, using ingredients that would make her roll over in her grave, either laughing hysterically or shaking her head in disbelief.

Any creative character can draw on their skills of invention; it's one of the gifts of creativity in all its forms. Think about athletes who invent moves or tactics to win their games. They string together the most extraordinary feats of physical prowess mixed with magical serendipity and timing to score the winning point or take the lead in a race. Often those things aren't something that can be trained for, as they're a combination of timing, placement and innovation.

A footballer can invent a movement or tactic in a split second to respond to something in the game. A director can invent a new way to effectively manage their favourite social or work gathering.

Think about where in your life you most use your skills of invention and innovation. Finding where your inventing abilities lie will help you discover your creative character.

Chapter 5

Creative character quiz

This brings us to the play personality quiz. If you've read the questions at the end of the play-personality chapter, by now you should have a pretty good idea of which style of play and creativity suits you the most. In the quiz, there are eight different personalities with ten questions for each. Tick or mark the circles that remind you of the way you behave socially, at home and at work. At the end, calculate your highest score out of ten, and the second and third highest-scoring personalities as well. These will be your primary play personalities.

A combination of your highest-scoring personalities will make up your creative character. Engaging your creative character in your life is like being in your element. This is where you find the most success in accessing your creativity, innovation and connecting with Your Inner Knowing. Remember, none of these play personalities are fixed, and you can move through all of them at different times in your life. If you go to my website (www.yourcreativesuccess.com) you can do this same quiz and see a pie chart of exactly how you score for the different play personalities that make up your creative character. There is also a lot more information on the website at the end of the quiz about how these connect you with your creativity.

THE JOKER

- ☐ You love to play pranks and practical jokes
- ☐ You play the class clown
- ☐ Your stories make people laugh
- ☐ Your favourite kind of entertainment is comedy (films/sitcoms/stand-up)
- ☐ You can remember a lot of jokes
- ☐ You tell a lot of jokes
- ☐ People often comment on how funny you are
- ☐ You'd rather laugh than be serious
- ☐ You always see the funny side of situations
- ☐ Your career/vocation involves making people laugh

TOTAL

THE KINAESTHETE

- ☐ You need to move in order to think
- ☐ You prefer physical activities over sedentary ones
- ☐ You've always loved playing sports or physical games
- ☐ Sitting still for hours is difficult and you like to get up and move
- ☐ You like to push and test your body to see what it can do
- ☐ You take good care of your physical body
- ☐ Your career/vocation involves being physically active
- ☐ Your friends and family describe you as being sporty and healthy
- ☐ You like to keep fit
- ☐ When you go on vacation, you're not one to spend hours lounging around

TOTAL

THE EXPLORER

- ☐ You love to travel to new places, physical, mental, emotional or spiritual
- ☐ You love to try new things
- ☐ Your family and friends describe you as being adventurous
- ☐ You thrive on experiencing the wonder of discovery in your daily life
- ☐ You dream of discovering new things in your chosen field
- ☐ You always seek to find out more than the what's already present
- ☐ In your chosen career/vocation, you're at the forefront of innovation & discovery
- ☐ You'd rather explore something new rather than what's tried and true
- ☐ You're sure life is full of undiscovered wonders and potential
- ☐ Your exploration takes you beyond everyday life to a place where there are fewer to share the experience with

TOTAL

THE COMPETITOR

- ☐ You love to keep score
- ☐ You've got a lot of trophies/medals/certificates
- ☐ Your friends and family describe you as being competitive
- ☐ You are committed to being the best
- ☐ You reach your goals
- ☐ You have great focus and discipline
- ☐ You succeed in a highly competitive environment
- ☐ You love to be number one
- ☐ You excel at things when winning something is involved
- ☐ You always hold a senior position in family/work/social situations

TOTAL

THE DIRECTOR

- ☐ You love to plan and organize things
- ☐ You love giving directions (but might not take them very well)
- ☐ You love to be the organiser at work, family or social situations
- ☐ People often call on you for help when they're having trouble getting things organised
- ☐ Your career/vocation involves planning, organising and orchestrating
- ☐ You have great planning and organising skills
- ☐ You love to make up agendas and delegate
- ☐ You could organise a successful garden party in a blizzard
- ☐ You thrive on the importance of being the key orchestrator/organiser
- ☐ If something is badly planned or organised, you always know how you can do it better

TOTAL

THE ARTIST/CREATOR

- ☐ You love creating something from nothing
- ☐ You gifted at creating things or making things work
- ☐ Your career/vocation is in a creative field
- ☐ Your friends and family comment on your creativity
- ☐ You spend hours tinkering with something just for the fun of it
- ☐ You love to make anything that is beautiful, unique, quirky or functional
- ☐ Other people copy your original and creative ideas
- ☐ You lie awake at night thinking of countless creative ideas
- ☐ People come to you for advice or assistance with creative tasks or things
- ☐ You very skilled at coming up with new ideas and unique ways of doing things

TOTAL

THE COLLECTOR

- ☐ You have a cupboard, room, garage or yard full of something that you keep getting more of
- ☐ Your career/vocation involves collecting or being around collectors
- ☐ You swap and trade things for items that are very similar
- ☐ You buy and sell things with other collectors
- ☐ You socialise with other people who collect the same thing
- ☐ You go on trips or holidays just to get more of whatever you collect
- ☐ You collect experiences of a certain kind of thing and keep a record of them
- ☐ Your friends and family joke about your ever expanding collection
- ☐ You spend a lot of time looking on ebay for more of the things you don't need but you love having more of
- ☐ You can fill in this sentence 'She/he who dies with the most——wins!'

TOTAL

THE STORYTELLER

- ☐ You love telling stories
- ☐ When you tell stories, your audience is captivated
- ☐ You have a vivid and active imagination
- ☐ Your friends and family comment on your amazing imagination
- ☐ You get completely immersed in films, books, games or performances as if you become part of the action
- ☐ You are a performer or speaker
- ☐ Your career/vocation involves some form of telling stories
- ☐ You can convey things very effectively to others through stories
- ☐ You loved reading chapters of novels for homework when you were at school
- ☐ You understand the inherent power of stories and storytelling

TOTAL

Part 3
The great advocates of creativity

" When we express our creativity
we take on the role of inspirational
leader. We don't have to think
about this in our creative process;
it's just a matter of course that our
creativity will inspire others.

—*Neroli Makim*

Chapter 6

Why creativity is so important

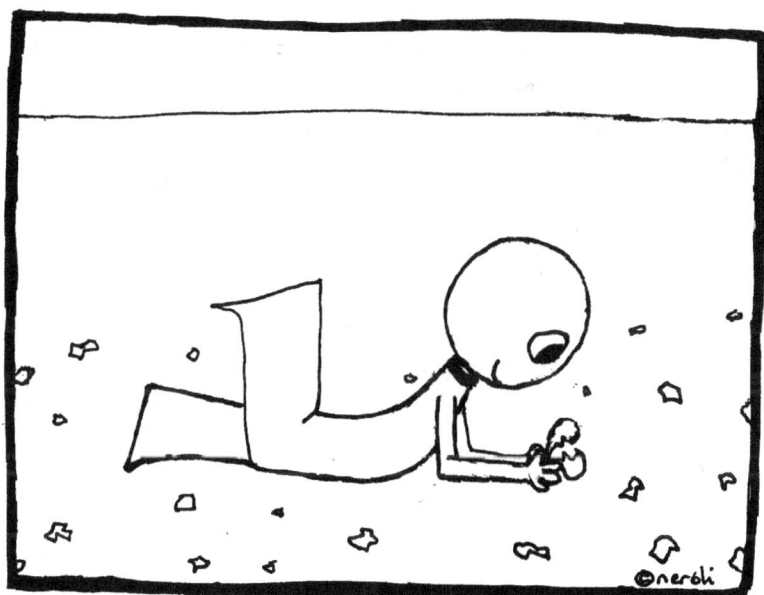

I must warn you that at this stage the book becomes quite serious in its referencing of experts on creativity. For the first few chapters it was more like we were just having a leisurely chat, but I can't just tell you why *I* think creativity is important if I want you to take it seriously. It's time to hear from the experts (we'll go back to leisurely chatting after we've covered the whys of creativity).

In an earlier chapter we learned how Dr Brown was drawn to examining the importance of play after the Charles Whitman case. Although this was an extreme example of why it's so important to include free play (which is a major component of creative expression) in our lives, Dr Brown's work continues to uncover how integral it is for healthy development in each of us. He states that play lies at the heart of creativity and innovation, and both are critical elements in our happiness and ability to sustain social relationships.[27]

Dr Brown notes that creative expression in the arts promotes community integration and interaction: 'Art is part of a deep, preverbal communication that binds people together. It is literally a communion. Creativity is important because it can put us in sync with those around us and enables us to tap into common emotions and thoughts and share them with others.'[28]

Our creativity and play help us interact with others and make us feel part of an integrated social structure. Another way of explaining it is to say that our creativity helps us fit into a group, tribe or community. We need to find our own unique place in our respective tribes; being accepted and included in our chosen tribe or community is a crucial part of feeling secure and belonging in the world. Our unique forms of creativity and play help us find our place in our tribe.

Sir Ken Robinson considers creativity to be of the utmost importance at this stage of our life on Earth. He says: 'We have no idea what's going to happen in the future … no idea. Nobody has a clue what the world's going to look like in five years' time, yet we're supposed to be educating our children for it.'[29] This brings to mind an aspect of creativity as 'imaginative processes with outcomes that are original and of value'. The extreme rate of change happening in all aspects of life on our planet means we'll need a lot of original ideas and creativity to help us navigate this future we haven't got a clue about!

Your Inner Knowing, your play personality, and inspiration from others all provide you with the creative problem-solving skills needed to deal with life's challenges. In order to access and fine-tune these skills, we need to recognise the importance of play and creativity in our lives and the lives of our children. Allocating time and energy to creative play is the key to dealing deftly with life's ups and downs. Remember, when the going gets tough, the tough go out to play!

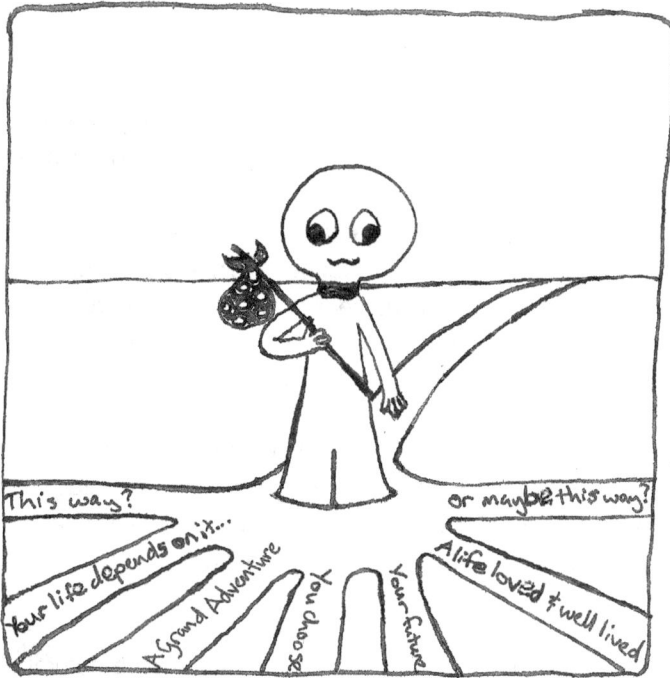

According to Sir Ken, a big part of the challenge we're facing is our lack of trust and confidence in our creative ability. He says: 'We've been educating people out of their creativity … We've been educated to become good workers rather than creative thinkers … Our education system has mined our minds the way we strip mine the earth for a particular commodity, and for the future, it won't serve us.'[30]

Sir Ken's findings are supported by the following example Dr Brown writes about in his book regarding a situation at JPL, the United States premier aerospace research facility for over seven decades.

In the late nineties, Cal Tech's Jet Propulsion Laboratory (JPL) found that the new engineers they were hiring to replace those who had been at the frontiers of the aerospace industry since the 1960s were incapable of certain types of creative and innovative problem-solving; they lacked the ability to translate things from a theoretical to a practical level. It didn't matter that JPL was hiring the best engineers from the most prestigious engineering schools in the country – a major component of the new recruits' skill base was still missing. JPL was alerted to the fact that a lack of play and creative investigation in childhood games was the cause of the new recruits' diminished creative problem-solving skills and inability to put theory into practice. In other words, the older generation of engineers had engaged in free play in their childhood years with more frequency than the younger engineers. Like little kid engineers at play, the older generation of engineers had used their hands, pulling apart, building or fixing things. It's precisely this kind of play and creative investigation that helped them become brilliant aerospace engineers![31]

The way we've been educated in recent times may be severely handicapping our creative and innovative abilities if we haven't been encouraged to engage in free play and creative expression. As the above story illustrates, play and creativity are vital elements in our ability to access the innovative problem-solving skills needed to carry us through life.

Even if you haven't been playing a lot lately, you were a natural at it when you were a child. Play has a way of creeping into your life through any little crack or crevice it can find. Your Inner Knowing is always with you, and your play personality is forever hanging around nudging you to join in the fun. It's pretty easy to get the ball rolling again and find your element. Once you find it, you'll want to be in it a lot more of the time. And when you're in your element, sparks begin to fly and your creativity whizzes into action with the same joy and enthusiasm you felt as a child.

> The great news is, Your Inner Knowing hasn't gone anywhere. It was with you when you were born, and it's with you until you die.
>
> —*Neroli Makim*

It seems that each child's unique form of creativity and play is paramount to their ability to identify a career that they love and excel in as an adult. Sir Ken calls this 'finding your element'. Our creative play history seems to be of service to others while being ultimately rewarding and fulfilling for us as well.

Many years ago I had the pleasure of working for a gifted film composer and amazing woman, Rachel Portman. I remember her telling me about being the youngest child in the family. She was often at home with no one to play with as her siblings were significantly older and away at school. In order to pass the time on those long, dreary, drizzly days in the English countryside, she would play the piano, losing herself for hours in her practice. Rachel's childhood play and creativity have rewarded her with being the first female composer to win an Oscar, and she was recently given the prestigious appointment of Officer of the British Empire (OBE) for her contribution to the arts.

As far as my own creativity being of service to me, the value and benefits of being blessed with a childhood that gave me plenty of time for free play and creative expression are extraordinary. Would you believe that when I was a kid I would draw pictures to illustrate stories to relieve boredom? This book couldn't even exist if it hadn't been for my childhood creative play. My entire gamut of creative expression owes itself to being given a lot of free-range creative play.

When I was about eight or nine, my mother bought a hand-held video camera. It was in the days when they were still very big and clunky, but we thought it was amazing! My older brother, sister and I got hold of it and made A.N.D Productions. This was an acronym of our names: Airdrie, Neroli and Dominic. We did spoof news reading, with the kind of reporting kids wanted to listen to rather than the stuff aimed at adults, and we made weird, kid-humour advertisements for toothpaste that tasted like dogs' droppings.

One of my childhood chores was watering the garden. I liked doing this because it made me feel peaceful and I enjoyed tending the plants. Nowadays I find I can access some of my best insights while spending time in the garden, and being around plants is calming for me. Spending twenty minutes or half an hour relaxing in the sunshine is the best holistic therapy I've found. It totally clears up any stress or anxiety problems I have, as it always lulls me into a dozy sleep like some kind of magic ray! All these activities that I did intuitively as a child assist me in adult life to deal with daily challenges and take care of my health.

We often spent an entire day on horseback mustering cattle, or travelling on long car trips, and I learned to drift off for hours in my imagination to pass the time. These days, my imaginative and creative visualisation skills are vital to every aspect of my creativity. I'm especially content when it comes to spending time alone, mulling over ideas and floating in and out of the stillness where YIK lives.

We've covered some fairly major aspects of why creativity is not only important but absolutely necessary for the healthy formation of the rich and diverse tapestry of life, both individually and collectively. We've looked at the dictionary definition of creativity, and our ability to bring the unknown and unseen into the realm of the conceptual perception so that we can understand it. We've also looked at how play and creativity hold the keys to our evolution, both individually and collectively.

I've also noticed that through my creative expression that I can access certain insights and concepts that are often well beyond my current level of understanding. This means my creativity can access wisdom within me that can be far greater than anything in my current, conscious reality. Eventually, when I decipher the intuitive guidance in my creativity, the information I glean from it helps me make sense of the world I live in. It also assists me in navigating through my life and relationships.

Now I'm going to tell the story of some of the challenges I faced in my stubborn inclination to play and be creative, and how, ultimately, it all worked out.

Often, the artworks I make are completely intuitive and I have little or no idea of the significance of what I'm doing at the time of making then. There seems to be a time lag of anywhere from six weeks to six years, or even longer, before I realise what my Inner Knowing was trying to tell me about myself and the world. There's a perfect example of this time lag in a later chapter, where I talk about learning to fly.

This tendency to make things without knowing why got me into all sorts of trouble when I was at art college. For the first time in my life I was told I had to know what, how and why I was creating. In other words, I needed to bring a sequential, linear element to a process that I had never experienced as remotely sequential or linear before, and this caused me no end of puzzlement. I was given the impression, in no uncertain terms, that 'inspiration' was a dirty word, and 'intuition' didn't seem to be recognised at all: it was not in any way a valid explanation for how an artwork came into being.

I distinctly remember the concept of inspiration gathered intuitively from some internal world, especially a spiritual one, being treated with significant scepticism, suspicion and possibly some ridicule.

This posed a very perplexing and in some ways humorous problem for me. Here I was, being told I had to go about and find proof of only the external influences for what I was doing and map my creative play like some kind of finely planned and completely comprehensive process.

Of course, this seemed absolutely illogical and impossible to me, because I couldn't map out journeying into the unknown, and dissecting and planning my creative play was like giving a flight plan to a butterfly I'd just dissected and asking it to take flight. Working like this really helped some students but this style of creating killed my process completely. For my whole life, I had just been playing creatively because it was fun. Although I didn't realise it at the time, it had helped me make sense of the world, both internally and externally. My creativity and play helped me feel an empathetic connection to all of life.

This is all very well, being able to articulate this clearly now after years of grappling with why and how I navigate the world in the manner I do, but back in high school and university I had no idea. I'm sure I just came across as an annoying and immature student. I never read the project briefs properly and would always go off on tangents of my own, getting far too absorbed in my own creative play to even consider what the point of the exercise was.

Inevitably, when the work was critiqued, while mine may have seemed unusual and interesting it rarely covered the required criteria. I remember so many of my poor, well-meaning teachers and lecturers looking so frustrated and exasperated with this seemingly capable student who just wouldn't read briefs and follow instructions, and even worse, didn't seem to care about them that much. It's true, I didn't care, even though apparently I was meant to care about getting good grades and passing. I'll talk about this in relation to creative expression shortly.

I'll never forget Craig Walsh, an accomplished and talented artist who had the unenviable task of assisting us figure out how to articulate our creative process and the subsequent work for final grading. When he asked me why I was making all these clay figures, I responded, 'I dunno, I'm just making them.' At which point he laughed with tentative amusement and said, 'Ummm, okay. Just don't say that in your critique.' Then he kindly attempted to help me find ways to make sense of what I was doing.

There's another extremely interesting facet to this story of my tussle with myself. My creative process worked but didn't fit into the protocols of the education system. The art pieces I started to produce at university began to express my struggle and subsequent feelings about my life in a very clear and explicit manner.

Instead of making individual works, I started to make figurative moulds of the same human form, over and over again. One work consisted of figures in a very restricted form, a lot like people in straightjackets, and each one was covered with a variety of materials, looking very restrained and even tortured. The work I made as my graduation piece for my university degree spoke volumes. Soon I was making hundreds of little clay figures in a manner very similar to that of a worker on a factory production line. The manner in which I was creating bore a striking resemblance to Sir Ken's words about being educated to become a good worker rather than a creative thinker. The figures looked like empty shells, devoid of any substance, spirituality or individuality.

What stunned and amazed me about this particular work is how those same empty and lifeless figures transformed into a powerful and vibrant expression of the cycle of life after I followed an intuitive hunch to place them in a certain formation several months after leaving university (see image on opposite page).

This highlights another extraordinary element of your creativity: it's as fluid and metamorphic as your own consciousness. It can literally transform into something else entirely as your mind shifts through different levels of awareness, evolving with you. Over the next ten years I gradually gained a complete comprehension of the message within the artwork and was then able to share this understanding with others.

The reason I didn't care about my grades or my schooling much was that a part of me never understood the point of most of my education, and therefore I never took it seriously. This same part of me was desperately grappling with and trying to reconcile with the mystery of life.

So far, not much about life made sense. My insecurity about all this uncharted territory and my inability to navigate it stopped me from engaging with it fully. It

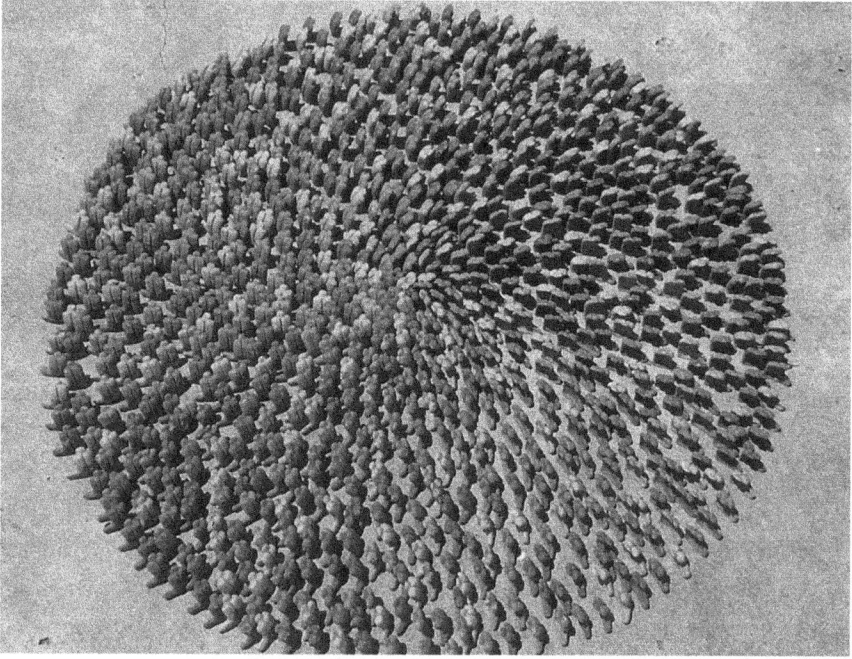

From a distance, this artwork looks like a pile of dirt. Upon closer inspection, it is still a pile of dirt, but shaped by hundreds of tiny human forms. Apart from slight variations in tone, shape and size, these forms are identical, in much the same way humans are. Age, race, gender or creed does not define these figures. They all flow in the same direction, following the same cycle of life. This mass of humanity is how I perceive our human experience. Like the clay forms, our bodies are shells housing our spirit. We are made of physical matter, like the earth. We come from the earth, literally. From our first to our last breath, directly or indirectly, the earth feeds us, nourishes us and gives us life. We are very much a part of the earth, and our bodies will return to it upon departing this life. No one escapes this cycle of life; we all come full circle in the end.

—*Neroli Makim*

seemed more important that I find my unique road map for life and learn how to read it. Somehow, I intuitively knew that my play and creativity combined to make up this map. That's what I needed to concentrate on.

I know of three educators whose work is, I believe, vital to creating awareness about effective education for adults and children. I'd like to share with you a little about them and their work.

Dr Stuart Brown is an author, speaker and the founder of the National Institute for Play. He consults and speaks internationally on the importance of play in our lives and the serious consequences if it is neglected. As you've probably noticed, I've referenced Dr Brown extensively throughout this book.

Sir Ken Robinson works on a global scale to catalyse a revolution in our education systems and businesses. His goal is to ensure that creativity plays a central role in our learning process. This is necessary in order for us to access the gifts that are vital to our health and wellbeing, as well as that of our planet and its future. The only way any of us will learn to read our own map and access our gifts is through engaging in the kind of creativity and play that we're naturally drawn to in the game of life.

Dr Demartini is a human behavioural specialist, educator and author. He has worked in diverse education and business environments helping people connect their values (which is another way of saying their play and creativity) with their daily lives. When we can see valid and meaningful reasons for what we're doing, we feel inspired to engage in the process.

Dr Demartini has found that when a child's values (play and creativity) are connected to their schooling, they begin to appreciate and engage in the learning process. This is when scholastic abilities and achievements blossom.

Now that I understand how my unique creativity and play process works, and why and how it is valuable, it's easy to share my gifts with the world. This benefits my community and myself. Any learning or work I do nowadays is connected to my play and creativity so it's a pleasure to do it instead of a drag. This is how we get paid to play!

Part 4
Intuitive creativity

> The joy of self-expression is undeniable. We can feel it bubbling up from within and it bursts forth in a happy little babble of creativity.
>
> —*Neroli Makim*

Chapter 7

Cultivating your creativity

The three chapters in this section are all about the ways in which you can cultivate the creativity that already lies within you. Common complaints regarding creative expression are that we feel blocked, uninspired or incapable, and that we don't have the time, energy or money to nurture our creativity. In this first chapter I explain how some of these blocks manifest in our lives and give strategies for overcoming them.

The secrets to creative success already lie within you; it's just a matter of accessing them. Often the ways in which you cultivate your creativity have little to do with adding more to yourself and a lot to do with clearing the clutter. Creativity will flow more completely once you've cleared away some of your fears, insecurities and excuses to allow your wisdom to surface. I'll share with you some of the things that have helped me and others improve our quality of life dramatically, our connection to YIK and our creative insights and expression.

Of course, there are infinite ways to cultivate one's own creativity. Because each of us has a unique blend of play personalities and values, cultivating creativity is a personal journey of finding the activities you feel naturally drawn to. These will be activities that give you a sense of joy, pleasure and fulfilment while challenging you to stretch beyond your comfort zone for even greater personal discovery and evolution.

It all begins with something small

Being afraid to begin the adventure is the foremost thing that can block you from getting started; it stops a lot of us from taking that first step. The fact that we must all begin small is so screamingly obvious that I wonder if it needs to be said at all, but I like the drawng on the opposite page so much I'm going to say it anyway!

Think of anything that you've ever created and you'll find that it never began with some giant explosion onto the scene. More than likely the final product was the culmination of the many and varied elements of your life experiences and skills colliding, presenting you with a little treasure.

Don Tolman is a fascinating, insightful and entertaining authority on holistic health and self-education. He describes this aspect of creativity wonderfully: 'Even the mightiest oak was once just a little nut that held its ground.' Imagine a beautiful, majestic oak tree. It certainly didn't grow like that overnight. Like your creativity, it began life as a tiny little seed, full of potential!

Good examples of little seeds full of potential are two extraordinarily creative and inspiring entrepreneurs: Sir Richard Branson and Oprah Winfrey.

Richard Branson's first business was creating a little magazine called *Student* with his friend, Johnny Gems. After leaving school the two men lived and worked in a basement, sleeping on the floor. Nowadays Sir Richard is a billionaire who flies to the moon and has two of his own islands. Oprah Winfrey started out at a small, local radio station in Nashville, Tennessee. Nowadays she is also a billionaire. She owns her own production company, and is cited as being the most influential woman in the United States, if not the world.

Today Sir Richard Branson and Oprah's creativity is expressed on a global scale, affecting the lives of people across the planet. As you can see, neither of them started out ranking in *Time* magazine's top 100 most influential people on the planet. They both began just as small and unnoticed as anybody else. Sir Richard and Oprah are great examples of individuals who planted the seeds of their creative inklings. Having demonstrated that they are worthy recipients of life's gifts, they have created ever more opportunities to express and experience their unique style of playing and creating.

The point of these stories is that we don't need to go looking at all the big things people have created and think, 'Oh no! They're all too big and good and how can I ever start unless I can make something as big and good as that straight off?' It's problematic that we're so accustomed to getting things at the touch of a button, because we often expect all of life to work that way. Then we get annoyed when we're reminded that it doesn't.

Everyone's creations began with something small and seemingly insignificant to most of the world. What matters is that your tiny creative inkling is important enough for you to nurture it into something that lives and grows with you for as long as you'd like it to. Remember, we all get some tiny little seeds of creativity to sow in the beginning. As we continue to use our creativity, proving to ourselves and others that we are worthy recipients of life's gifts, we get more opportunity to experience and express our creative genius.

Is there an example in your own life where you've taken some small and seemingly insignificant idea that you've been playing around with and put it into action? Then found that you're given more opportunities as a result of this little creation, and it has grown and evolved into something bigger and more wonderful than you could have imagined?

Slow and steady

The first two lines of the following qote are from the Bible, found in the book of Ecclesiastes; the words are attributed to King Solomon, 900 BC. The rock 'n' roll band The Byrds forever immortalised these lines in their song, 'Turn! Turn! Turn!' The wisdom in these words is as relevant today as when they were written by King Solomon in 900 BC or when sung by The Byrds in the sixties.

To everything there is a season, and a time to every purpose under Heaven.

—*Ecclesiastes*

Trust in this and act on Your Inner Knowing. It will all come full circle in the end and you will begin the cycle again.

—*Neroli Makim*

If you try to rush or alter the natural growth process of a plant, or tamper with it by adding artificial chemicals or stimulants, you can interfere with the integrity of its cell structure. You may produce an inferior-quality fruit, seed or flower, damaging the soil in which you hope to grow more plants in the future. The same can be said for your creative process. If you try to rush it along and ignore the rhythm of your life's natural creative process, you may end up with compromised creations and a shoddy foundation for your future creative endeavours.

This book did not spring onto the page in a matter of weeks. Although I put the thoughts, words and images together in a few months, the ideas and inspiration had been incubating away within me for a lifetime. I drew the following picture eight years ago.

A series of drawings in a later section under the heading 'Learning to fly' were penned about the same time, in response to my sister's relationship breakup.

This book really *is* the creative expression of my thirty-four years of life experience and skills colliding and presenting me with this little treasure. There's no way this little treasure could have been made if I'd tried to rush the process and scrawl out a book about creativity when I was twenty-four. A huge amount of creative inspiration and insight available to me now were not even on my radar at that stage of the game.

If you trust the creative process that follows Your Inner Knowing's organic rhythm and your life's natural cycles, you can take a lot of the stress out of your daily life. Your creative expression doesn't need to happen at the push of a button; even if it did, it would make for a very dull and boring creative experience. Each person's rich, inner world is defined by the experiences that form the threads of their individual maps for life.

Information overload and creative stagnation

Before we look at why an overload of stimulus from our external environment can hamper creativity, it needs noting that creativity also thrives on external influences. Inspiration from others is a vital part of the creative process. The problem lies in the fact that sometimes all the external stuff can end up taking up all the space available. This leaves no room for you, especially if you're not finely tuned in to your own creative element.

Living in an urban environment, our senses are smashed with hundreds of images, words, sounds, colours, smells, conversations, questions and concepts on a daily basis. Even living in a remote or rural environment, with television and the internet, it's easy for one to be subjected to a huge quantity of external stimulus. It's almost impossible to avoid being the target of some kind of sales pitch and marketing campaign. Given that the essence of our creativity are the inklings of our inner world bubbling to the surface, it can take some serious attention on our part to make space for them amidst all the clutter.

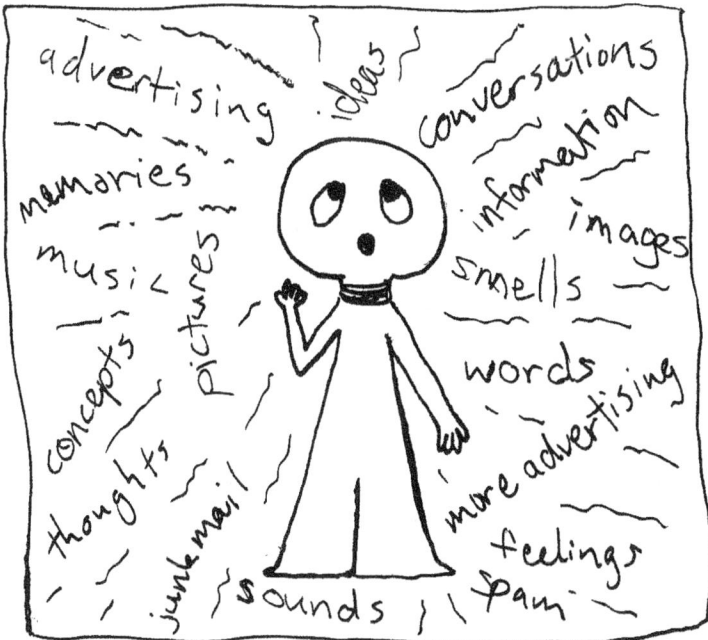

I've heard people say that the only thing that can never be taken from us is our mind and the choices we make with it. Even this real estate is up for grabs in most of us, particularly in children. It has been well documented that a child's mind is like a sponge and soaks up huge amounts of information in its developmental stages. The space in our minds is preyed upon by anyone who wants us to pay attention to something that's important to them.

All this stuff that we're being given information about may not be very life enhancing at all, although it certainly fills up and clutters our mental space on a daily basis.

If you'd like to test yourself to see just how little of your mind and its thought processes you really own, try spending just ten minutes of your day when you're driving somewhere in a town or city without taking in any external information (except what's absolutely necessary for safe and responsible driving). You'll find that you can't have the radio on, as it will inevitably have people chatting at you about all manner of things that lead your mind off on various tangents. You can't look at billboards, as your thought processes will be led off in a direction predetermined by the advertising pitch, and just glancing at shop fronts can hijack your mind with whatever it is they're promoting. Even reading bumper stickers can take your thoughts off on some trajectory or another.

In fact, it's almost impossible to spend even a few minutes in your car resting your mind from external stimulus. You never get the opportunity to see what thoughts arise from within you rather than from someone else's prompts. People often experience a false sense of power, autonomy and privacy when driving their cars (think nose-pickers and pushy road-ragers), but by doing this exercise you will see how very little power, autonomy and privacy you actually have if your mental environment is constantly at the whim of external stimulus.

If you don't drive, this exercise can just as easily be done on a train or bus, or while walking. One of the reasons people listen to or repeat affirmations is to manage the input and content of their minds so that they're in control of what's happening in there. Reading a book or listening to music while commuting accomplishes the same thing.

With such sensory and information overload, it's no wonder people often feel exhausted and overwhelmed at the end of a day's work. I haven't even begun to take into account the time and energy spent with family and friends after work. Information overload and the huge demands on our time, energy and attention can easily overwhelm even the most seasoned creatives among us. We think we've never got the time, space, energy or money, and this is one of the major causes of never planting the seeds of our creative inklings.

We are all someone else's target market – from birth until the day we die.

—*Neroli Makim*

Learning to fly

Learning to fly is something you experience within, rather than read about, so the next few pages are going to be mostly pictures with little bits of text to guide you along – then a bigger splash of text to finish. But for those seeking to realise their creative potential, I hope the following pictures and text play a big part in finding your element and staying in it.

Most of us have experienced some kind of challenge and heartbreak in our lives, whether it's a physical, emotional, mental or spiritual challenge. Experiencing some pain and challenge is a normal and healthy part of growing and maturing as a person. It helps us to learn and develop skills and abilities navigate the ups and downs of life skilfully. The late Joseph Campbell, a mythologist, writer and lecturer, said, 'Follow your bliss! … But if your bliss is just fun and excitement, then you are on the wrong path. Sometimes pain is bliss.'[43]

This natural process of experiencing both support and challenge helps us develop and evolve. This gets jammed when we haven't seen that there are actually significant benefits and blessings in these painful and challenging experiences. The benefits and blessings are a bit like angels sent to help us appreciate and integrate this pain and challenge into our lives, making us who we are today.

Instead of seeing the blessings or benefits within the pain and challenge, we can sit there, stuck in overwhelming hurt. It stops a part of us from moving on. In fact, if we haven't recognised the benefits and blessings of the situation, a part of us is still sitting there; a part of us is frozen in the painful memory. This interferes with our ability to see the situation completely and fully appreciate the gifts inherent in it. We always receive some gifts and benefits as a result of experiencing pain and challenge.

We may be so oblivious to the benefits of the pain and challenge that we don't even notice them. The trick is to become aware that experiencing pain and challenge facilitates the realisation of our innate gifts and amazing creative potential.

Eventually, life will make it so we can't ignore the situation any longer. Then we may begin to see the angels of blessings and benefits. It's up to each individual to decide if they want to learn to fly. People and circumstances are there to help us, but only we can decide if we want to heal the parts of ourselves that are frozen in painful memories. When we decide this, we've earned our wings and we're ready to fly!

Then we have lift-off! YAY! Hurrah! Fabulous you! When you begin to see the benefits and blessings of your life's painful and challenging experiences, you literally feel lighter, and your heart begins to soar. The weight of the pain, guilt anger or despair you've been carrying in those memories dissipates when you can see how those same experiences have made you the wonderful person you are today, and when you become present to the amazing gifts and abilities that you have had to develop as a result of them.

This leads us to the splash of text at the end of these pictures …

If some part of you is frozen in the memory of a challenging experience, it can seriously hamper your ability to feel your heart. If your heart is closed, the transmission lines to Your Inner Knowing are disconnected.

Creative inspiration, expression and play need to be connected to work. If there's a part of you stuck in memories from a painful past, it's going to be very difficult to live to your full potential – to do so you need a full and open heart, not a broken one.

In 2001 my younger sister had gone through a very painful breakup with her partner. The experience gutted her and her life fell apart temporarily. At the time I was practising Vipassana meditation for two hours every day. For those of you unfamiliar with Vipassana, or insight meditation, it is a type of meditation developed by the Buddhists to assist in the experiential understanding of the fleeting nature of things. The type of insight meditation I practised focused on a profound and present awareness of bodily sensations.

During this time, I experienced great clarity of mind and connection to my Inner Knowing. I made a card for my sister, with little pictures similar to the ones you've just looked at. Somehow, these little scribbles made sense of her experience. They illustrated for her something within herself that she had previously been unable to articulate. She told me: 'When I looked at the pictures, for the first time I knew everything was going to be all right in the end.'

In 2006 I encountered the work of Dr John Demartini. I heard him do a one- or two-hour presentation on stage during a four-day workshop that was packed with other speakers. The concepts and information he gave me in that short time were enough for me to decide immediately to go on and study more of his teachings.

The reason I was so interested in learning more about his work was because the essence of what he spoke about was in the scribbles I had given my sister six years before (this is the example I mentioned that demonstrates how your creativity can access your own inner resources of wisdom). During his life's work, Dr Demartini has explored more than two hundred different disciplines in pursuit of what he calls Universal Principles of Life and Health.

A primary focus in his work is the balance of polarity: balancing good and bad, light and dark, pain and pleasure, and so on. Dr Demartini says: 'Even the most terrible events always contain hidden blessing. Love is made up of two sides: support and challenge. We're required to experience both sides equally. One of the greatest illusions people fall into is the search for pleasure without pain, praise without reprimand, or nice without mean. Looking for illusive, one-sided events in a two-sided Universe is the root of people's so-called suffering.'[44]

Dr Demartini's teachings are supported by the words of Joseph Campbell, whom I referred to earlier. If you remember, he said: 'If following your bliss is just fun and excitement, then you're on the wrong path. Sometimes pain is bliss.' Interestingly enough, one of the greatest cyclists and sportsmen in history shares the same philosophy. A reporter asked Lance Armstrong what pleasure he found in riding his bicycle for hours. Lance, seven-time winner of the Tour de France, had difficulty comprehending the question. Finally he responded: 'I didn't do it for pleasure, I did it for pain!'[45] It was through the pain that Lance was able to enter into the state of presence that allows us to experience the transcendent beauty of both polarities balanced in oneness. My brother, father and late grandfather experienced this same phenomenon in long-distance endurance rides.

I have found Dr Demartini's work invaluable in helping me decipher my own unique map for life and awaken to my creative potential. He's a truly interesting and gifted individual.

Is there anything in your life you've always wanted to be, do or have but for some reason you have held back from taking the plunge and going for it?

When you're searching to rediscover your unique creative gifts and play personality, the process can often be hampered by fears and guilt from past experiences. This may block you from allowing yourself to truly shine and have the life you deserve. It can also block you from ever taking that first step and planting the seeds of those creative inklings.

Is there an experience in your life that has been very challenging, but when you're able to look back on it you know it gave you some of the greatest gifts and strengths that you are truly grateful for now?

Perhaps this challenging experience marked a big turning point in your life. Often challenges take us on a new path that is ultimately very rewarding.

I've had the series of pictures from 'Learning to fly' made into an animation; it comes to life on a whole new level with music that was composed especially to go with the story. You can see them if you look me up on YouTube or go to my website (www.yourcreativesuccess.com).

If the little pictures and story from in this section touched your heart and stirred within you an inkling to understand more about the laws of support and challenge and both sides of love, I would thoroughly recommend you go along to listen to Dr Demartini speak. Luckily, he spends nearly every day of the year travelling all over the world speaking and presenting, so wherever you are you should be able to catch him on a stage near you. You can find more information about Dr Demartini, his work and his whereabouts by looking him up online and going to his website (www.drdemartini.com).

Chapter 8

Supercharging your energy and inspiration

L ack of time is a common block we come up against in our lives and it can interfere with our creative adventures if we let it. If you can assign big blocks of time and resources for your creativity and play, brilliant! If, like many people, your time is splattered with disruptions – and you can't lock yourself away from them all and turn off the phone and internet for a few hours – just work in between the distractions. This is not the ideal way we'd all like to go about our creative play, but it's better than giving up on it altogether.

Speed-training creativity

Think of all the mothers who have to master the juggling act of accomplishing things in between distractions all day long with small children. They do it, and not just for a day but for years! You can do the same with some practice. If that perfect, still, silent space in which to practise your creativity is something that never makes its way into your day, please don't use that as an excuse to ignore Your Inner Knowing telling you to plant the seeds.

You can learn how to squeeze in ten minutes of creative play between other tasks and appointments. This is because you are training yourself to consciously drop out of the world of external distraction. You can also learn to access your play personality and inner wisdom with far greater dexterity and ease than if you always had perfect blocks of stillness and silence in which to do so.

The downside is that with such small windows of opportunity, you may only scratch the surface of your inner world. You may have quite a strong blend of external stimulus in your creative playing, but it's amazingly valuable and rewarding all the same. When we're engaged in creativity and play, we experience continuation desire. This means we enjoy what we're doing and want to keep the fun going, so it's easy to keep up the momentum and come back for more later. Even ten minutes of creative play can give us a boost of the refreshing and revitalising energy of joy, pleasure, freedom, and the satisfaction of taking a micro-holiday.

Remember, your creative play doesn't have to be a big deal. We don't have to get everything perfect just so we can make a start. If we fall into this trap life will have slipped through our fingers before we've had the joy of even one creative adventure.

Hugh MacLeod scribbled on the back of business cards while waiting for his friend or date to show up for a drink after work. Rather than waiting for the time/space/money to begin planting the seeds of creativity, he just did it. Now he's a published author, successful businessman and creative entrepreneur. Above all, Hugh has found a way to express his creativity without watering it down to suit someone else's agenda. By sneaking in little scribbles of creative play wherever he could, Hugh found his element. His creativity doesn't depend on the approval or assistance of any external authority. And that, ladies and gentlemen, is a beautiful example of what dancing to the beat of your own heart looks like.

There are, however, some other lovely and enjoyable ways to help maintain your energy and inspiration besides trying to squeeze creativity into the crevices of an already crammed life. I cover these in the following pages.

Juggling creativity with your life's distractions takes you to a different level of mastery.

—Neroli Makim

Learn on the go

A great thing about your creativity is that apart from being able to enjoy it with little or no money, you also don't need experience or training to be creative. Creativity is an innate part of your being, and you can learn on the go. In other words, you learn through the process of doing. It can be a far more enjoyable and rewarding way to learn. This process is often referred to as: *Fake it till you make it*. If you trust that you can learn on the go, it's less likely that you'll get caught in the trap of thinking you need to know everything before you begin your creative adventures.

In the year 2000, I made an entire wearable artwork out of sticks I picked up off the ground and butcher's string I pilfered from my parents. This particular artwork won $1000 in prize money in an internationally acclaimed art show and was purchased by the gallery for their permanent collection for another $1500. I had just returned from an overseas trip so I was quite happy to pick up the spare cash. I didn't spend a cent on the materials (my parents were short some string though!). I had no formal training in weaving natural fibres, and nor did I have any kind of special preparation before making it. My education in weaving natural fibres came from looking at some pictures of baskets in a book when I was at university, then I figured it out as I played around with the materials. (You can see a picture of this artwork on my website: www. yourcreativesuccess.com.)

Of course, if you're going to design and build a bridge that carries the traffic of a city's population on it, money, training and experience are not only important, they're essential. If you just want to play around and experience the joy of creativity, all you need is the desire to do so, a few small bits and pieces to make it happen. Then take action!

Another example of learning on the go happened to me recently. After reading the Ringing Cedars series of books, a friend and I were inspired to grow some of our own food and strengthen our connection to the earth and nature's cycles. I'm lucky because I felt no great need to get any special training or skills. I just started planting seeds and experiencing great joy as I watched them sprout up out of the ground a few days later. Over the past few months, in keeping with the creative process I outlined in an earlier chapter, my garden has grown from a few little pots into an astonishing variety of garden beds of all sizes. My gardening skills and knowledge grew to accommodate my increasing desire to potter, plant and play with growing things.

It can be a tricky dance, dodging creative stagnation, information overload and avoiding over-education. Often we need some education and information, just not to the point of being overwhelmed by it. There's nothing wrong with learning new things and getting special training either; I do it all the time. But as far as your creativity goes, a lot of it is trusting and acting on Your Inner Knowing. Then you can naturally grow your skills in tandem with your creativity. You can then revel in the joyful pleasure of watching your creative inklings sprout as a result of taking action.

We can learn, read and study all we like, but it won't get us an ounce closer to actually experiencing our own creativity and finding our own truth until we take action and plant the seeds of our creative inklings.

Can you remember an experience when you were faced with a situation where you just had to figure out a way to deal with it and use whatever skills and resources you had available to you at the time? Have you ever had to fake it till you made it? These are times when you have been engaging your creative skills in a big way and learning on the go.

> Being creative involves doing something … you cannot be creative unless you are actually doing something … creativity impacts the public world.[46]
>
> —*Sir Ken Robinson*

Abundance is everywhere

Now, before you go off on a tangent, thinking this is some New Age hype pitch, it isn't! Abundance is everywhere in an external sense if you look for it, but particularly within you as far as your creativity is concerned. What gets in the way of us experiencing this abundance of creativity within us is our own conditioning. That is, we're just not accustomed to recognising how clever and creative we really are. I'm going to tell a story that demonstrates just how locked into our habitual responses we can be. The story also shows how this stops us from recognising the abundance around and within us.

> If we were more accustomed to looking around for where this abundance is, instead of where it isn't, we would find it a lot more often.
>
> —*Neroli Makim*

The other day I was outside feeding the chooks on a rainy day. I was having a lovely time, scattering chook food on the ground and enjoying the sound of the raindrops splashing on the umbrella canvas. When it was time to go inside, I found I had quite a grubby hand from holding the dusty grain. I looked around for the garden tap to wash it off. I even went so far as to turn on the tap when I realised the ludicrous irony of my actions.

Here I was, standing in the pouring rain, and there was enough water falling out of the sky to wash the whole city, not just one grubby hand. And I was about to turn on a *tap* to wash it! I laughed both *to* myself and *at* myself, a little embarrassed at how habitually conditioned my actions were and how removed I was from my commonsense and practical observational skills.

This is how many of us can go through life: locked into habitual patterns of thinking and behaving. In doing so, we miss the abundance of ideas and opportunities available to us. Our physical, mental and emotional habits keep us locked into thinking and acting in ways that not only confine our creativity but block it altogether.

I mentioned earlier how our creativity is amazingly fluid and metamorphic and reflects the energy of our minds. I had been making a whole lot of human forms that looked hollow, dejected and lifeless. When my thoughts changed about my life experience, the artwork took on a new, vibrant expression about the cycle of life.

Think about when you've changed your mind about something. Most of us will have experienced times when certain thoughts or judgements we're holding have been turned upside down. This is great, because it shows us that our minds are not completely locked into our habitual patterns. Nothing is fixed and all things change and transform.

We experience so many thoughts and feelings in just a few minutes. Your creativity is the same. It can flip, change and transform in accordance with your own consciousness. So the more you allow your mind to remain open to the abundance of creative possibilities and potential within yourself, the more you will experience it in your life. The way your creativity works is through inquisitive play, exploration and experimentation. If you are following the same repetitive, robotic responses in you actions or thinking, then you will miss the endless opportunities for creating and experiencing something new and different.

In order to change this habitual response pattern, all you really need to do is observe yourself in your daily life. In much the same way as I caught myself, just as I was about to turn on the tap, you can also observe your thoughts and actions. See if you're following a habitual pattern and check to see what other options there are and if they serve you better. Either way, any attention you give to the way you live your life will bring more conscious awareness to it and open up new possibilities. By observing your thoughts, actions and responses, you will break the cycle of living mindlessly and begin to live more consciously. From a place of conscious awareness, you can really begin to create instead of letting your habitual responses bounce you off everyone else's creations. Practising a form of meditation that suits your play personality can assist in strengthening your observational skills.

Both my exploration of still meditation (Vipassana) and moving meditation (yoga) has helped me become more mindful of my thoughts and actions. What types of play or creative activities have you found that help you become aware of the way you respond to life and open up new possibilities? Your Inner Knowing gifts you with insights into your creative potential. Each of us has our favourite ways that help us see these possibilities.

True food nude

True food nude is real, whole food, grown in healthy soils by ecologically sound means; food produced without excessive use of processing, preserving, or manufacturing techniques that make it more like a science experiment than food that comes from the earth. This section may seem a little out of place in a book on creativity, but it's essential in managing your life in a way that will allow you to have the time, energy and money available to enjoy and experience your creativity to its full potential. You may have all the energy in the world when you're loving what you're doing and being paid to play, but if you don't take care of your physical body, you won't have the vehicle to enjoy it.

Like the section on why creativity is important, I do quite a lot of referencing here. There are many distinguished experts in the fields of food, health and nutrition whose work I reference. I do this so my readers are aware that I'm not just making up random facts to support my way of thinking.

You are the most qualified person to make choices and decisions about what works best for your own health and nutrition needs. I am not a nutritionist or trained medical doctor and I recommend you always seek professional medical advice before following any of the tips given here.

If we take a look at the time, money and energy equation, energy rates as a major factor in living a full and prolifically creative life. If we're malnourished, we certainly won't have the energy we need to cultivate our creativity; instead we will need to spend more of our time and money on propping up our health as it fails from lack of good nutrition.

It's easy to take note of how you feel after eating and drinking certain things. This helps us discern which foods and drinks make you feel healthy and energised, and which ones leave you feeling sluggish. Can you remember an occasion when you've felt really alive, healthy and energised?

For me, these memories equate with times I've taken care of my health and nutrition needs, and felt creatively inspired.

Can you imagine even considering making time to connect with Your Inner Knowing or play personality if you're suffering from some kind of illness or degenerative disease? Even though doing this can be very beneficial to our healing process, when we're sick, most of us can only spare the time and energy to focus on just getting through the day. A lot of stress-related illnesses and degenerative diseases can be prevented with good nutrition and eating habits.

Most of us think malnourishment is a Third World disease. If we live in a place where we can easily access as much food as we like, we're pretty sure we aren't suffering from malnutrition. However, according to Dr Victor Zeines, a holistic dentist and nutritionist with twenty-five years of practice, we're lucky if we're getting maybe forty percent of the nutrition we need from today's food.[33]

Many of the things we eat and drink in Western society don't really resemble the food grown in nature that's beneficial to our health and provides for us nutritionally. Many processed foods are often combinations of manufactured chemicals, textures and flavours masquerading as food and drink. The problem is, these things do such a good job of pretending to be food that we eat and drink them and think we're doing okay. Charlotte Gerson of the Gerson Institute says: 'Even if we are eating a lot of commercially grown fruits and vegetables, if the soil they're grown in is deficient in trace elements and minerals, and toxic with chemical pesticides and sprays, we can't help but be deficient and toxic as well.'[34]

There is a lot of debate over whether this is true or not, and it really is up to the individual to decide for themselves what works for them, through their own observations of their health and diet. What I've learnt from those who live on the land and observe and study the link between the health of our land and the health of our bodies coincides with my own research and experience. There is a growing body of scientific research that shows we are destroying Earth's ability to sustain and nourish us; destroying our physical and mental health and the future of life on this planet by poisoning the soil, water, plants and animals through the use of chemical fertilisers and genetically engineered foods.

For further, detailed information on this topic, I recommend Andre Voisin's book, *Soil, Grass and Cancer*. This book was first published in 1959, and the observations, information and insights contained in the book are a testament to the author's visionary creative gifts.

Eric Schlosser spent three years studying the American food industry, and in particular the fast-food industry, while researching his book, *Fast Food Nation*. During his research, he studied the makings of processed and packaged foods and what makes them taste so good that we not only eat them but go back for seconds. Advertising psychology aside, it seems to come down to two main reasons: flavour and mouthfeel.

If a scientist doesn't get the texture/mouthfeel and the flavour right, it's a big waste of the food company's time and money because no one's going to buy a packet of crisps that feel and taste like cardboard. Without the scientist's skills, a lot of processed food could be just like that. According to Schlosser, if you look on the packaging of almost all foods in your fridge, freezer and cupboards, you will probably find 'natural flavour' or 'artificial flavour' on them.[35] Almost all processed foods need to have chemically manufactured flavour added because the techniques used to make processed food destroy most of the natural flavour.

Schlosser says: 'The distinction between artificial and natural flavors can be somewhat arbitrary and absurd ... A natural flavor is not necessarily healthier or purer than an artificial one (consumers prefer to see natural flavours on a label, out of a belief that they are healthier). Flavors are created by blending scores of different chemicals in tiny amounts ... the job of the flavor scientist is to conjure illusions about processed foods and ensure consumer likeability. In order to give processed food the proper taste, a flavorist must always consider the food's mouthfeel – the unique combination of textures and chemical interactions that affects how the flavor is perceived. The mouthfeel can be adjusted through the use of various fats, gums, starches, emulsifiers and stabilizers.'[36]

Back to the question of how all this affects our creativity. If we're eating mostly a combination of artificially manufactured chemicals and textures, we're most probably not getting the nutrition our body needs from them. Professor Ian Brighthope says that if we eat junk food for one day, we're going to be massively deficient in a whole range of nutrients, and that's just one day. We cannot punish our cells without having to pay or it, sooner or later.[37] Our body can buffer us from stress and toxins for a while, but not forever; the devil gets his due, eventually. There's no point creating an amazing life if we haven't maintained the physical vehicle to enjoy it.

If we're eating a diet of highly processed and packaged foods, then it's very possible we're suffering from malnutrition to some degree. If we're suffering from malnutrition, we feel depleted just fulfilling our daily tasks and responsibilities. We'll be hard pressed to find the energy for our creative exploration and expression. Unhealthy eating habits will eventually drain more of our time and money into saving our ailing health.

But wait! Don't despair! I know very well that not everyone can access, afford to, or even want to live on fresh, organic produce. In fact, many people may not have the resources or access to such lifestyle choices or the desire to change their eating habits so dramatically. Most importantly, Your Inner Knowing is the best guide for you to make choices and decisions about food and diet.

You know which eating habits benefit you the most. I love food and cooking, and I want to have my cake and eat it too! Thankfully, I've found a perfectly simple and user-friendly remedy to the problem to ensure I'm getting enough nutritional value in my daily diet: superfoods! Yay!

You will have heard of most of the ones I'm going to list; including them in your diet is like chomping on multivitamins. Taking vitamin supplements can also be a beneficial alternative, although it can get tricky knowing which ones actually contain nutrition that the body's cells can recognise and absorb easily, as well as knowing which ones are being manufactured in a way that's conducive to the goodness getting through to you.

With superfoods, we can buy them in their raw, natural state so our body can recognise and assimilate them as it would any other natural food that it's designed to assimilate. They're mostly dried and sometimes processed into powder for preservation and easy conversion into liquid form. This enables super fast assimilation into the body.

Spirulina, macca or raw cacao powder are good examples of superfoods that you can drink and are very high in vitamins, minerals and antioxidants, and help boost energy levels.

I have a few favourites that I include in my daily eating habits and they keep me humming along brilliantly. There is no way I could accomplish as much as I do if I didn't keep my energy levels up with superfoods throughout the day. When I don't take care of my health, I usually hit a mid-morning or after-lunch slump where I feel like lying on the couch and having a little nap, and that's all very well except sometimes that luxury is not even a remote possibility.

I've experimented with many types of eating choices. I grew up eating a diet that included a lot of naturally produced, grass-fed red meat, I've been vegetarian, and I've spent a while eating just raw foods. At this stage in my life

I prefer to allow myself a little of whatever I feel like eating, along with aiming for at least fifty-one percent of raw food in my daily intake. That's not that difficult if I have fresh fruit or a smoothie for breakfast and salad with lunch and dinner. I top up with a few superfoods each day to balance out my love of all things tasty but that are not so healthy.

The best news of all is that our bodies, like the environment, are amazingly effective at healing. The way to right the wrongs of malnutrition is as simple as chowing down nutrient-dense foods and superfoods. Compared to becoming very ill and relying on drugs to keep us going, nutritional medicine is cheap, it's simple, it's safe, and it's effective.[38]

The other great news is that superfoods are easily accessible at your local health-food shops or via the internet, and there's a wide variety to choose from, so if you don't like one superfood there's sure to be plenty more to chomp on. We have a number of amazing superfoods grown here in Australia, and some, like the Kakadu plum, are native to this country.

Again, choosing what works for you is going to be something that only you can decide. Your Inner Knowing is a great guide when it comes to figuring out what your body needs for its optimum health and wellbeing. You know yourself better than anyone else ever can, so trust in your own instincts when it comes to choosing the foods and eating habits that work best for you. Here is a short list of some of the heavyweights in the superfood spectrum:

goji berries	coconuts
cacao	kep
maca	Kakadu plums
bee products: honey, pollen, propolis	camu camu berries
spirulina	aloe vera
hempseed	

If you would like more information on these superfoods, their nutritional value and what the benefits are of taking them, you can find plenty of information on the internet. For more detailed information on diet, nutrition and the way your food is being farmed and produced I would thoroughly recommend you pick up a copy of the DVDs *Food Inc* and *Food Matters*.

Food Matters was produced by nutritionists-turned-filmmakers James Colquhoun and Laurentine ten Bosch. It combines the knowledge of leading medical experts around the world and covers some very simple yet vital aspects about food, nutrition, good health, and preventing and reversing chronic health conditions. Watching *Food Matters* is one of the fastest, easiest ways to get very clear and concise information about your diet and nutritional needs that will serve you for the rest of your life.

Food Inc was produced by award-winning filmmaker Robert Kenner and investigative journalist Eric Schlosser, whom I've referenced extensively in this chapter. It is an extremely insightful film that shows you just how the food that reaches your table is being produced and how that's affecting your health and the health of your family. You can find both DVDs on the internet.

This brings us to the third and final chapter in this section: The hidden path to Your Inner Knowing. The following ideas and exercises need to be tailored to suit your individual play personalities' that way they become thoroughly enjoyable and easy to accomplish.

Chapter 9

The hidden path to Your Inner Knowing

In the final chapter in this section we look specifically at ways to facilitate a greater connection to Your Inner Knowing and unlock the secrets to your creative success.

Take a hike!

Next time someone tells you to 'take a hike' don't be offended; they may be giving you some very sound advice on how to access your creativity and improve your life.

One of the great philosophers of our time, Friedriche Nietzche, said: 'All truly great thoughts are conceived by walking.'[32] Taking a walk is a *great* way to clear your mind from unnecessary clutter and give your energy a boost. Walking can help you get in touch with Your Inner Knowing, as well as having a multitude of health benefits.

A study by the National Cancer Institute published in the *Archives of Internal Medicine* proved that people who take a thirty-minute walk five times a week increase their health and longevity. Studies also show that walking increases your energy levels, and improves concentration, memory and psychological wellbeing.

When you take a walk you're moving your body, which was Robert Fagen's remedy for filling an empty heart. You're also removing yourself physically from the life situations that are cluttering your mental, physical and emotional space. If you're walking in a park or somewhere a little removed from the many pollutants of city living, you're getting a cleaner, clearer mental and physical space to contemplate your creative inklings.

For the price of twenty or thirty minutes in your day, you can give your soul some space for contemplating your own creative expression. During this time, you can gain valuable insights into the best course of action to take in expressing these creative ideas. JK Rowling says there's nothing better for clearing the head and getting inspired than going for a stroll in the evenings.

Let's go back to those three pesky reasons we give ourselves for why we can't or won't be more creative: lack of time, lack of money and lack of energy. Taking a hike is one way of cultivating creativity that addresses all three of them.

If we feel we don't have enough energy, going for a walk has been shown to *give* us more energy. If we feel we don't have enough time, it's only twenty or thirty minutes three times a week. Given that, on average, people find the time to watch four to five hours of television a day, or play on the computer, then it's only a matter of taking eleven percent of that time and channelling it into increasing your energy and creativity. As we've discovered, walking will give you more energy anyway, so you won't need as much downtime in front of the tube.

Finally, walking is *free*! Woohoo! We don't have to pay any money to anyone to go outside and take a walk. We don't need any special equipment or attire. Even if you only own six-inch stilettos and cocktail dresses, you don't have to go and buy special walking shoes or clothes. Walking can be done in the nude and in bare feet! (But I wouldn't advise this unless you're wandering around in a nudist colony.) Most of us can find the appropriate attire and can enjoy a gentle stroll through the park.

But I know walking is not going to be everyone's cup of tea. While it's a free and relatively easy way to gain many benefits, there are other ways that we can connect our Inner Knowing and play personality, so let's have a look at some of them …

Get out of town

This creativity-enhancing technique can cost a bit more of your time, energy and money, but the benefits are well worth it. When you take a walk you can remove yourself briefly from your everyday responsibilities, concerns and distractions but getting out of town means removing your self from your daily roles and responsibilities for a much longer period of time.

I advocate going someplace else entirely. (For me that's preferably somewhere quieter and closer to nature.) When you remove yourself from the rituals, roles and demands of daily life, you can clear your head, rest your body and listen to what your heart and soul have to say to you. Getting out of town means removing yourself from your everyday roles and responsibilities long enough to reconnect consistently with Your Inner Knowing and engage in some of your favourite ways to play.

During the writing, editing and rewriting process of this book, I have been truly blessed to be able to take myself to my parent's farm to spend a few weekends just focusing on my creativity. As soon as I get here, I relax in the quiet and sleep so soundly in comparison to my noisy, city home. By removing myself from the endless distractions of my usual living environment, I get a lot more quality work done.

Besides being nurtured in a warm and loving home (for the last two days I've been tucked up on a big comfy chair with my laptop next to a deliciously warm fire), the silence and stillness of the pristine countryside make it easy to focus and allow my creative thoughts and insights to surface. I find they flow more consistently and fluidly than they do when competing with sirens, traffic and the constant external stimulus and distractions of urban life. Have you ever noticed this in your own life's experiences? When you take a break and leave your everyday roles and responsibilities at home, have you found you feel more relaxed and open to your creative insights and wisdom?

I find that one day away is barely enough but better than nothing; two days away is getting closer to clarity; three days away and my creative inklings and inner world stirrings are easily accessible and discernible.

The more time and space you can have away from your daily life's concerns, the more clarity, perspective and insight you can gain about Your Inner Knowing and the secret language of your own soul.

Have you ever wondered why Carthusian monks choose to live a life of quiet contemplation in relative solitude? They choose to live in this manner because it removes them from as many of the distractions of daily life as possible. I find that silence is one of the best ways to create and maintain a connection to my Inner Knowing and commune with my heart and soul. Of course, vows of silence and hours of contemplation are not to everyone's taste, so the rest of us can just take a few mini-breaks here and there to reconnect with ourselves and recharge our creativity.

Another good reason to get out of town is that the constant pollution of urban living is something we grow so accustomed to that we don't even notice it's there. But our body notices it, and our mind notices it. There's pollution in the air we breathe, the mental environment we live and work in, the things we eat and drink, and the sounds that fill the city day and night.

To see what kind of toll this pollution takes on you, try lying down somewhere comfortable and going through your body, consciously relaxing all the tense muscles in your neck, back and shoulders, then throughout the rest of your body. Most of us go to sleep at night without spending the time to consciously scan through our bodies and see how it's reacted to the day's events. Usually, as you lie there, you'll find some extremely tense muscles. Some of these will let go as you consciously breathe into them and imagine them releasing tension. Others are so well locked up that they're going to need a lot more help to relax fully.

When I go for a massage, I'm usually shocked at how stiff and sore my muscles are. They've been holding that stress and tension the whole time without me noticing because I'm so distracted by everything else I'm busily attending to. These tense muscles are an example of the way our body is noticing and reacting to the stress of life and the polluted environment around us.

What often happens when we take time out and remove ourselves from our everyday roles and responsibilities is that we get sick. Or we're just wiped out and need to rest intensively for the first few days of our break. The body and mind are finally able to relax and let go of some of the tension and toxins we've been holding onto for weeks, months or even years. The stress on the immune system causes the body to become ill for a couple of days. It's not such a bad thing, as it forces our body and mind to take a rest for those few days; it's just our way of internal housecleaning. This demonstrates how the body is impacted by the strain of our everyday lifestyle. Our body can hold the effects of this stress within us and buffer us from it while we go about living it, but only for a while. We are humans, not machines, and it catches up with us if we don't give ourselves downtime.

The exercise I recommended you do in an earlier chapter to observe how much external influence and stimulus you encounter in ten minutes is a great way to see how the external clutter affects your mind. If you had trouble spending even ten minutes moving through your environment and keeping your thoughts free from external influence, imagine what state your mind is in at the end of every day. We spend our days taking in so much external stimuli that we really do require some time out from it occasionally.

As mentioned earlier, getting out of town isn't as easy to accomplish as going for a walk. It will cost more of your precious time, energy and money to organise but it does offer far greater rewards for the effort made to do so, as a rest and recharge does wonders for connecting to Your Inner Knowing and accessing your creative insight and expression.

The greatest players on Earth

It always helps to learn from the best, so they say, and coaches are always telling us to surround ourselves with those who are already brilliant at the things we aspire to. Well, when it comes to play and creativity, this means taking lessons from children … and animals too. Most people who own dogs will attest to their playful nature. Robert Fagen spent ten years studying the intricate play behaviour in wild bears.

If you really want to observe creative genius in action, sit quietly and observe free-wheeling child's play. Picasso said: 'All children are born artists, the problem is to remain an artist when we grow up.'[39] If you've had a look at the link to the amazing stories of Miss Capucine that I referred to in the earlier section on the storyteller play personality, you would have seen how imaginative and inventive a child's creativity can be. Now let's have a closer look at why children are so adept at playing and creative expression.

Children generally aren't afraid of launching themselves completely into a creative endeavour or game. Most children will take a chance more readily than most adults. Because of this, they experience and express their creative potential more easily than we do.

Our schooling system, and society in general, doesn't reward us for making mistakes or for time spent playing. This really does throw a big spanner in the works, because our ability to make mistakes and engage in free play helps us become amazingly creative individuals. We need to re-educate ourselves to be okay with making mistakes, and learn from them.

Dr Brown repeatedly finds that clients who have lost their sense of playfulness in their daily lives experience ever-deepening despair and depression instead of waking up with a feeling of joy and inspiration at the break of each new day.

And once again, if you look at the greatest players on Earth you'll see that most small children don't have any trouble waking up to greet each new day with joy and enthusiasm. Every child I know aged four and under loves to wake up and charge out of bed to launch into the adventures of the new day. Much to the dismay of many tired parents, the little creative genius they've brought into the world thrives on waking around dawn and getting busy with the day's creativity and play.

My parents were taking care of my niece and two nephews while my brother and his wife were away for the weekend. Just as the first rays of daylight began to creep through the bedroom window, my niece sat bolt upright in bed and called out to her grandmother: 'Wake up, Ninny! I see the day!' Then she prised Mum's eyes open so she could 'see the day' too! Of course, a very weary but doting grandmother fumbled out of bed and headed out into the

> If you don't know, have a go. If you're not prepared to be wrong, you'll never come up with anything original.
>
> —*Sir Keith Robinson*

frosty morning to join the little one in feeding the chooks and letting the dogs out of their kennels. Meanwhile, a very grateful grandfather huddled under the covers, glad that one doting grandparent was enough to accompany the boundless enthusiasm of a three year old.

For five years I worked as a children's program facilitator at one of the major art galleries in Australia, and I've worked with children for over ten years. During this time, I've observed the extraordinary capacity for creative expression and imaginative play in most children. I've observed how much joy and energy they derive from this freedom. I am constantly amazed and humbled by the originality and authenticity of children's creative expression.

Whilst facilitating children's art programs, I would often see the adults chaperoning the children becoming absorbed in the creative activity and leave looking even more refreshed and revitalised afterwards. It was as if suddenly they were given a little loophole in their daily lives to let loose and play with some glue and paper or coloured paint, crayons and pencils. This is something that most adults will rarely or never allow the time for in any normal daily schedule.

Hugh MacLeod says: 'Everyone is born creative, everyone is given a box of crayons in kindergarten … being suddenly hit years later with the creative bug is just a wee voice telling you, "I'd like my crayons back please." Your wee voice didn't show up because it decided you need more money or you need to hang out with movie stars. Your wee voice came back because somehow your soul depends on it … so listen to your wee voice or it will die … taking a big chunk of you along with it. They're only crayons, you didn't fear them in kindergarten, why fear them now?'[41] (Love your work, Hugh)

If, as adults, we were able to recapture only a fraction of this freedom that we had as children to play and create I'm convinced we would feel more energised and fulfilled as we went about meeting the responsibilities of our daily lives. 'What might seem like a frivolous or childish pursuit is ultimately beneficial. It's paradoxical that a little bit of "nonproductive" activity can make one enormously more productive and invigorated in other aspects of life. When an activity speaks to one's deepest truth, it is a catalyst, enlivening everything else.'[42]

In regard to Your Inner Knowing and creativity, think about when you were a child and the kind of play activities you loved and could spend hours doing. Can you remember which types of playing and creativity you could become so immersed in that it caused time to disappear?

These are elements that link you to your unique blend of play personality and creativity. I would often read or draw and write little stories because it helped me fill in the hours during the day when it was too hot to play outside. As an adult, these are still some of my favourite ways to connect to my Inner Knowing and engage my creativity.

> Most of the things that are really useful in life come to children through play and through association with nature.
>
> —*Luther Burbank*

Give everything

Like learning to fly, this aspect of cultivating your creativity is best said with a picture and as few words as possible. We touched on the importance of putting your whole self into your creative expression earlier when we looked at how the creative process works.

Give *everything*. It's much the same as Hugh McLeod said: 'Put your whole self into it, and you will find your true voice.' Giving everything means putting your whole self into your creative expression, to create from the heart. In doing so you find out who you are. You find your own truth, and you connect with Your Inner Knowing. This inspires others to do so as well.

Is there something you've done in your life that you poured your whole self into? Did it give you the most amazing sense of accomplishment and fulfilment, and inspire others as well? When we give everything, we feel complete and satisfied with our efforts. There is nothing anyone can say or do that can take away the sense of self-assurance we have when we know we gave it our best shot.

I'd like to add a small disclaimer here. I don't mean in any way, shape or form that you should go and pour your heart and soul into creative endeavours that involve giving everything to others without respecting your own time, energy, money or creativity. This may seem obvious for some people, but giving everything can be misconstrued as giving everything to everyone else but your self. That's a great way to burn out and get resentful and cynical. Giving everything also means giving to your self as much as giving to others. Whatever it is you decide to do creatively, give it your best and you will never feel like you've failed.

The passage opposite, which I wrote for no apparent reason a couple of years ago, sums up everything you need to know and remember with regard to creating authentically from your own inner beauty and wisdom.

Live, touch … give everything.

Begin now.

Trust in your truth and beauty,

then surrender.

Balance,

gratitude,

grace.

Love, laugh, play and dream.

Courageous wisdom, bless life free spirit.

Pure heart, question eternity.

Deep serenity, encourage energy flow.

Breathe. Feel. Believe.

Strong body, kind soul, inspiring light,

Give everything.

Look within so you don't go without

A significant block that can interfere with our creative expression is when we compare our selves and our creativity with someone else's. Hugh MacLeod calls it 'comparing your inside with somebody else's outside'.[47] This is a great way to miss our own gifts and accomplishments and diminish our creative ability.

When I was a kid I wanted to be as good as my older brother in everything because I thought he was really cool. The problem was, I was a year younger, and being a girl I couldn't match his physical strength, which annoyed me no end.

My grandfather, father and brother all used to go in these horse races called endurance rides. Sometimes, these races were 250 kilometres long. The riders started racing at midnight, rode all through the next day, rested that night, and then finished the race the following morning. When I was ten years old I went on my first endurance ride. Because it was only fifty kilometres long and I didn't win it like my brother, I never gave myself much credit for it.

When I was fourteen, I went in another race that was 160 kilometres. We woke up and rode from three in the morning until about seven-thirty that evening when I crossed the finish line. I had just come home from boarding school for the holidays and had been doing no training or conditioning for the race. Still, I gave myself no credit for this accomplishment, as my brother had raced in the 250-kilometre race when he came home from school on holidays at eleven years of age, and he won it – with a broken arm!

Now, as an adult, when I see kids aged ten and fourteen and they remind me of how little I was at the time, I think, *Wow! I can't believe I did that. That really was an accomplishment for a little kid!* But back then I was so busy comparing myself to someone else that I never stopped to even think that it was anything special, and this stopped me from acknowledging the gifts and abilities of my kinaesthete play personality.

Is there anywhere in your life where you compare yourself and your accomplishments with someone else? I'll bet that in doing that, you're ignoring Your Inner Knowing and obliterating some of your own greatness.

Feelings of lack can be one of the greatest hindrances to allowing our selves to live and create to our full potential. If we're holding onto any excuses as to why we can't follow our little creative inklings, it may have very little to do with the excuse we're telling ourselves, and a lot to do with our fears or feelings of lacking in some way.

These unhelpful fears make great partners in crime with excessive procrastination through endless diversions: study, learning, training and skill acquisition.

The truth is, when it comes to creativity you are abundantly creative and gifted already. You are a lot more capable than you give yourself credit for, and you can learn on the go, through your own experience. We don't have to build the Taj Mahal or create the next *Mona Lisa*.

Creativity is a game of playing, making mistakes, learning as you go and having fun while you're at it!

The best way to learn about your creativity and access your Inner Knowing is through play. You know what and how you love to play better than anybody else. Your creativity is your gift to the world and you were born with it. It's *your* creativity and *Your* Inner Knowing. This means there isn't anyone outside of you who can know more about your unique soul-print (USP) than *you*. The most someone else can do in regard to your creativity is point you in the direction of your self. I believe any teacher or authority that points you in a direction away from your self has no interest in you accessing your true potential or infinite wisdom.

We can find some amazingly gifted teachers, trainers, mentors and gurus, but really, they're our assistants. There are many great assistants out there who can hold signposts in the direction of your true north. I've sought the help of many an assistant to inspire me and keep pointing me in the direction of my own creative gifts. It's wonderful to have inspiring people around us who guide and assist us to learn and fine-tune the skills to access our Inner Knowing.

In much the same way that your life does not unfold within the confines of a clearly defined, linear sequence, your creativity does not follow a clearly defined, sequential, or linear path. 'Creativity is a process, not an event. Real creativity comes from finding your medium, from being in your element.'[48] Finding your medium is like finding the only map that exists for your life. By finding your medium, you find yourself.

Your play personality will direct you to your medium, and your play personality holds the keys to your creativity. When you are in your element, you are in a place of unwavering certainty and truth, even when the mystery of life engulfs you completely. Then you learn to swim in the mystery instead of flailing madly in the uncertainty, and this is the art of mastering you life.

When you've learned to listen to your own heart and follow the wisdom of Your Inner Knowing, you have learned to read your map for life. Then it doesn't matter when you reach the edge of that map. You've got the tools to go beyond the edges of your world and explore uncharted territory.

Creativity is easy. It's fun. You know how to do it. You were born knowing how. Let's play!

—*Neroli Makim*

About the author

Neroli Makim is an internationally acclaimed artist whose paintings and sculptures are held in both private and corporate collections. Her work has been exhibited nationally and internationally. Neroli's unique upbringing has had a profound effect on her approach to creativity, play and innovation. Creativity held the keys to filling the vast, empty expanses of a childhood spent in the remote Australian outback.

Her investigation into creativity led her to complete a bachelor degree in fine arts, exploring a wide variety of disciplines, including painting, drawing, photography, wearable art, and bronze, clay and fibre sculpture. Neroli's interest in the innate wisdom and creativity within each person led her to train extensively in the art of self-awareness and spiritual disciplines. Over the past ten years she has studied body-centred psychotherapy, moving meditation and Buddhist disciplines, and trained under select leaders in the field of personal development. Neroli's insatiable thirst for knowledge is responsible for her pouring an extraordinary amount of time, energy and money into her self-education, and she is a keen advocate of learning through personal investigation and experience.

An intense desire to understand more about the world, her place in it, and how the microcosm fits into the macrocosm and vice versa took her on a journey around the globe in her early twenties. From the isolated outback cattle station where she grew up, Neroli set off to immerse herself in the extraordinary art and culture of Italy. She lived in Ireland and London, and travelled around Europe before heading home via Russia, Mongolia and China. For the last five years she has been developing and facilitating art programs for private businesses while working in one of Australia's premier galleries.

Neroli's mission in life is to continue to explore and awaken the innate wisdom and creativity within her self and all those who seek to know their own inner genius. In her book, she reveals the simple yet powerful lessons she has learnt through her childhood experiences and extensive exploration of personal development and creative expression. This book is an ideal read for anyone seeking to experience greater personal fulfilment and creative success in life.

Notes

1. *The Australian Oxford Dictionary*, 2nd ed, Oxford University Press, UK, 1992

2. Ken Robinson, *Out of Our Minds*, Capstone Publishing Ltd, 2001 p. 118, p. 115, pp. 128–9, pp. 181–2

3. Hugh MacLeod, *Ignore Everybody*, Portfolio, Penguin Group, 2009 p. 44

4. Ken Robinson, *Out of Our Minds*, Capstone Publishing Ltd, 2001 p. 136

5. ibid., p. 181

6. ibid., p. 134

7. Hugh MacLeod, *Ignore Everybody*, Portfolio, Penguin Group, 2009 p. 82

8. ibid., p. 104

9. Jonas Salk, Ken Robinson presentation, 'Schools Kill Creativity', TED, http://www.ted.com, June 2006

10. Dr Stuart Brown, *Play: How It Shapes the Brain, Opens the Imagination and Invigorates the Soul*, Penguin Group, London, 2009, p. 5, p. 104

11. ibid., p. 203

12. ibid., p. 126

13. ibid., pp. 94–95

14. ibid., p. 29

15. ibid., p. 84

16. ibid., pp. 94–95

17. Ken Robinson, *Out of Our Minds*, Capstone Publishing Ltd, 2001 p. 131

18. Dr Stuart Brown, *Play: How It Shapes the Brain, Opens the Imagination and Invigorates the Soul*, Penguin Group, London, 2009 pp. 17–18

19. ibid., p. 66

20. ibid., pp. 66–7

21. ibid., p. 67

22. ibid., pp. 67–8

23. ibid., p. 68

24. ibid., pp. 68–9

25. ibid., p.69

26. ibid., p. 70

27. ibid., pp. 5–6

28. ibid., pp. 62–3

29. Ken Robinson presentation, 'Schools Kill Creativity', TED, http://www.ted.com June 2006

30. ibid.

31. Dr Stuart Brown, *Play: How It Shapes the Brain, Opens the Imagination and Invigorates the Soul*, the Penguin Group, London, 2009, pp. 10–11

32. Friedrich Nietzsche, 'Brainy Quote', http://www.brainyquote.com

33. Dr Victor Zeines, James Colquhoun & Lauren ten Bosch, http://www.FoodMatters.tv

34. Charlotte Gerson, James Colquhoun & Lauren ten Bosch
    http://www.FoodMatters.tv

35. Eric Schlosser, *Fast Food Nation*, Penguin Group, 2001, p. 120–1, pp. 128–9

36. ibid., pp. 128–9

37. Prof Ian Brighthope, *Food Matters*, James Colquhoun & Lauren ten Bosch
    http://www.FoodMatters.tv

38. Dr Andrew Saul, James Colquhoun & Lauren ten Bosch, *Food Matters*
    http:// www.FoodMatters.tv

39. Ken Robinson presentation, 'Schools Kill Creativity', TED,
    http:// www.FoodMatters.tv June 2006

40. ibid.

41. Hugh MacLeod, *Ignore Everybody*, Portfolio, Penguin Group, 2009 p. 28

42. Dr Stuart Brown, *Play: How It Shapes the Brain, Opens the Imagination and Invigorates the Soul*, Penguin Group, London, 2009, p.11

43. ibid., p. 202

44. Dr John Demartini, *The Breakthrough Experience*, p. 14–7

45. Lance Armstrong, *It's Not About the Bike: My Journey Back to Life*,
    Penguin Group/Penguin Putnam, 2000

46. Ken Robinson, *Out of Our Minds*, Capstone Publishing Ltd, 2001 p. 115

47. Hugh MacLeod, *Ignore Everybody*, Portfolio, Penguin Group, 2009 p .55

48. Ken Robinson, *Out of Our Minds*, Capstone Publishing Ltd, 2001 p. 129

www.ingramcontent.com/pod-product-compliance
Lightning Source LLC
Chambersburg PA
CBHW072012290326

41934CB00007BA/1067